SERGEI O. PROKOFIEFF (1954–2014) studied Fine Arts and Painting at the Moscow School of Art. He encountered the work of Rudolf Steiner in his youth, and quickly decided to devote his life to it. He became active as an author and lecturer in 1982, and helped found the Anthroposophical Society in his native Russia in 1991. In Easter 2001, he was appointed as a member of the Executive Council of the General Anthroposophical Society in Dornach, Switzerland, a position he held until his death. A popular speaker, he wrote numerous books and articles that are published in many languages.

CW00821034

RIDDLE OF THE HUMAN 'I'

An Anthroposophical Study

Sergei O. Prokofieff

TEMPLE LODGE

Translated from the German by Simon Blaxland-de Lange

Temple Lodge Publishing Ltd.
Hillside House, The Square
Forest Row, RH18 5ES

www.templelodge.com

Published in English by Temple Lodge 2017

Originally published in German under the title *Das Rätsel des menschlichen Ich, Eine anthroposophische Betrachtung* by Verlag am Goetheanum, Dornach 2011

A CIP catalogue record for this book is available from the British Library

ISBN 978 1 906999 97 1

Cover by Morgan Creative
Typeset by DP Photosetting, Neath, West Glamorgan
Printed and bound by 4Edge Ltd., Essex

Contents

Preface

At the request of a number of readers I have decided to publish the appendix entitled 'About the Inner Being of the Human "I"'[1] from my book on anthroposophy and Rudolf Steiner's book *The Philosophy of Freedom*[2] as a separate booklet. As the importance of this theme has been constantly reinforced in my mind, it seems appropriate to offer a more detailed study of it separate from the book referred to.

For this reason the text derived from the book has been incorporated without significant changes, although in order to facilitate a better overview it has been divided into two chapters. The third chapter has been especially written for the present publication. This additional content was a necessary means of providing the two previous chapters with the thematic completion which they merit.

The question of the nature of human individuality is one of the most important of all questions and is, moreover, one of the most difficult to answer; for it can truly be said that the nature of the ego is as complicated and many-sided as the entire cosmos to which man and his evolution belong.

Hence by means of this study my aim is to offer the reader not so much a simple solution of all the riddles associated with the nature of the ego but, rather, a deepening of this theme, so that what is under consideration here can appear in its full complexity and manifoldness.

For this reason the present publication will concern itself only with certain significant aspects of the whole theme. In Rudolf Steiner's legacy many additional facts and indications arising from his spiritual-scientific research on the ego can be found, the full investigation of which must be left to further studies of this subject.

1. The Threefold Nature of Human Individuality

Anyone who embarks upon the study of anthroposophy will soon recognise that the mystery of the human ego lies at its very heart. This mystery is one of the central questions of anthroposophical Christology and at the same time forms one of the most difficult cognitive challenges presented by anthroposophy.

When viewed from the standpoint of esoteric Christianity, the 'I am' aspect of the seven 'I am' sayings in St. John's Gospel is no mere grammatical formula but is the mystery name of Christ Himself. Rudolf Steiner once expressed this in very precise words: 'The true name of Christ is "I am"; anyone who does not know or does not understand this and calls Him by another name does not know anything about Him. "I am" is His only name' (GA 266/1, 27 May 1909). As has often been noted, the fact that the German word 'Ich' forms the initials of Jesus Christ is also an indication in this direction. Moreover, in the lecture of 11 October 1911 Rudolf Steiner speaks of how the human ego was as the result of the Mystery of Golgotha rescued for the whole future of world evolution (GA 131). It follows from this that the question of the nature of human individuality can be answered only out of its very intimate connection with the Christ impulse.

According to a report by Carl Unger (1878–1929), in response to a request to give a brief definition of anthroposophy in England for the Oxford Dictionary Rudolf Steiner wrote the following words in English: 'Anthroposophy is a knowledge produced by the Higher Self in man'.[3]

If a 'higher self' is referred to in this context, it follows that there must also be a 'lower self' (or 'lower ego'). Indeed, in virtually all of Rudolf Steiner's fundamental books one can find it in those passages where there are references to the path of inner development. In *An Outline of Occult Science* alone he refers to it in a variety of different ways: 'Earth ego', 'earthly ego', 'lower ego', 'ordinary ego', 'first ego'. In his lectures he gives it yet other names, for example 'transient' or 'ephemeral ego' (GA 112, 24 June 1909), 'the first self' (GA 147, 29 August 1913) and even 'physical ego' (GA 119, 29 March 1910) or 'physical self' (GA 10). This ego or self is from the outset associated with the physical body, whence its 'mortality' or transience arises. (Of course Rudolf Steiner does not ascribe any value to all these designations but merely identifies the relationship of the one ego that is accessible to our supersensible organs of perception to the spiritual (higher) world and that of the other to the physical (lower) world which reveals itself to our bodily senses.)

However, Rudolf Steiner also uses various names for the higher ego. The most frequent is 'higher ego' (GA 13), then 'second ego' (ibid.) or 'new ego' (ibid.), 'real ego' (GA 4, GA 35 and GA 187, 27 December 1918), or 'other self' (GA 17), 'spiritual ego' (GA 10), 'superordinate' or 'superior ego' (GA 16), the 'new-born ego' (GA 13) or the 'new-born self' (GA 13). He also for the most part uses the words 'ego' and 'self' as synonyms (see GA 10 and GA 13). All of this shows how freely he employed this terminology in his work.

The relationship of the lower to the higher ego and also the transition from the one to the other is of central significance to the modern path of inner development and is described at some length in *An Outline of Occult Science* and *Knowledge of the Higher Worlds: How is it Achieved?*. Especially in the latter book this process is explicitly compared to the birth of a child. Similarly in the lecture of 24 June 1909 Rudolf Steiner speaks of how 'within this [transient] ego another, higher ego is born, as a child is born from the mother' (GA 112).

Now it belongs to the nature of modern initiation that a person's ordinary or first ego fully maintains its earthly consciousness after the birth of this second ego, so that when the splitting of the bodily members comes about the life of the person concerned suffers no harm but is increasingly enriched. 'The split that has been characterised here is something of which one is fully aware *only* as a soul-experience, so that a sense of dwelling clearly and consciously in one's ordinary ego is in no way impaired. *This* "ego" loses nothing of its inner solidity and cohesion' (GA 113, 24 August 1909; italics Rudolf Steiner).

In his book *The Threshold of the Spiritual World* (GA 17), which was published in 1913, Rudolf Steiner for the first time introduces a third

ego and defines it quite precisely as the 'true ego'. Thus whereas the
higher ego or other self derives from the spiritual world, that is, from
the upper of the three worlds described in *Theosophy* (GA 9), the 'true
ego' must belong to a 'super-spiritual world'[4].

In spite of the unique definition of and distinction between these
two aspects of the ego in the lecture-cycle *Secrets of the Threshold* (GA
147), which was given in the same year, Rudolf Steiner frequently uses
the names synonymously. The explanation for this is that in certain
situations the true ego works through the other ego, so that they can
both be regarded as in effect a unity. 'We have pointed out that a
person can leave his astral body and be in his true ego. He will then be
living in the environment of the super-spiritual world. By entering this
world, he therefore finally gains access to what has always resided in
the depths of his soul, namely to his true ego; whereas he has in the
spiritual world already become aware of the way that the true ego, the
other self, manifests itself, that is, engirdled by a living essence of
thoughts ... This is what we really are, this other self, this true ego'
(op. cit., 31 August 1913). And in another passage from the same cycle
Rudolf Steiner indicates that it is only when one encounters the true
ego in the super-spiritual world that one also experiences the way in
which it was previously 'still ensheathed within the other self' (30
August 1913).

Rudolf Steiner also used the two terms synonymously in earlier
lectures. 'And what we normally experience as our ego, as our self,
amidst the physical world is not as yet our true self, it is not what we
call our higher self' (GA 113, 25 August 1909). Probably in view of
this great complexity of the nature of the ego, in his later lectures
Rudolf Steiner often uses the composite term 'ego-organisation'.

A threefold aspect can be distinguished in the inner structure of the
human ego, as it is described by Rudolf Steiner in the book *The
Threshold of the Spiritual World*. First there is our earthly ego-
consciousness, which is associated with the ordinary or lower ego and
which we receive as a result of our incarnation in a physical body.
'This ego-experience can become a reality for man in the world of the
senses only if he is engirdled by his physical, sense-perceptible body'
(GA 17, ch. 13). Then follows the so-called 'other self', also referred to

by Rudolf Steiner as the 'higher ego', 'which manifests itself in repeated earthly lives' (ibid., ch. 7). But man's spiritual centre is his 'true ego', or the divine spark within him. Only in his 'true ego' is he fully able to experience himself in the higher worlds as a spiritual being among other spiritual beings (the hierarchies). In the book referred to it is described as follows: '*The true ego in a super-spiritual environment. In the true ego man finds himself as a spiritual being, even when all experiences of the physical, elemental and spiritual worlds and, hence, all experiences of the senses imparted through thinking, feeling and willing sink into oblivion*' (GA 17, ch. 15; italics Rudolf Steiner).

If one now considers this process from the standpoint of world evolution one can say the following. The first or lower ego is merely a reflection of the 'other ego' that is working through it within the bodily sheaths. This latter consists of the ego-substance which the Spirits of Form—or, to be more precise, the seven Elohim dwelling on the Sun—sacrificed to mankind at the beginning of the Earth aeon. This occurred in the Lemurian epoch and formed the beginning of true *human* evolution on our planet. In the case of an ordinary person who is not an initiate, this 'other self' or higher ego does not enter the earthly sheath but remains behind at birth in the spiritual world. In the course of incarnation it sends from thence merely its reflection into the earthly sheaths, which a person then experiences as his individual ego-consciousness. Rudolf Steiner indicates this by means of the following words: 'You will say: so does a human individual today not also find his ego? No, he does not find it; for the *real ego* is immobilised when we are born. What we experience as our ego is only a reflection of the [real] ego. It is merely something that serves as a mirror-image of the pre-natal ego. We actually experience only a reflection of the ego; only very indirectly do we experience something of the *real ego*' (GA 187, 27 December 1918).[5] That these words concern man's higher ego follows from the fact that during earthly life it resides in the spiritual world and does not descend into earthly existence.

As for the 'true ego', there is at least one passage in Rudolf Steiner's lectures where there is a reference to its origin. In the cycle about the Book of Genesis (GA 122) he indicates that when the seven Sun Elohim decided to endow man with the substance of the ego, the forces that they had borne within themselves since primordial times seemed insufficient for their great intentions. As a result they established a new degree of union amongst themselves, and out of this created a new essence in the region of the Sun to which Rudolf Steiner gives the name of 'Elohimhood'. In this way they were able to rise to a higher stage in their evolution and receive an impulse from the highest sphere lying above the Seraphim, that is, above the hierarchic cosmos; for in order to imbue man with the ego as the central principle of Earth evolution, the seven Elohim had to receive the impulse for this from the *cosmic Word* itself as the mediator between the Holy Trinity and the world of the hierarchies.

Thus one can also say that every new creation in the universe begins with the second countenance of the Trinity, the divine Son, first manifesting Himself outwardly as the cosmic Word. He as it were imprints His innermost Being upon the world as the primal principle of procreation, as the all-creative Logos, the Word, of whom it is said in the prologue of the Gospel of St John that 'all things came into being through Him, and nothing of all that has come into being was made except through Him' (1:3; translation by Jon Madsen).

So there is not only a primal relationship between man's 'true ego' and the cosmic Word but pre-eminently a direct connection of this highest aspect of the ego to the Christ; for in Him the cosmic Word itself became flesh on the Earth and thus made it possible for mankind to experience *in the physical body* not only the 'other ego' (which could be achieved to a certain degree already in pre-Christian initiation[6]) but also the 'true ego'.[7]

This threefold structure of the human ego has its macrocosmic archetype in the mystery of the threefold Sun, which contains the secret of its union with the cosmic Word or, in other words, the transformation of the cosmic Word into the Sun Logos, which earthly human beings were later to call the Christ. In one of his esoteric Lessons Rudolf Steiner describes this threefold Sun as the 'physical, spiritual and Christ Sun' (GA 266/3, 18 May 1913). Thanks to the first Sun, which sends light and warmth to the Earth, human beings are able to develop ego-consciousness in their physical body. The dual influence of sunlight upon man's being gives rise to the realm of nature (outward aspect) and the etheric realm (inward aspect). Especially the second, etheric influence of the Sun comes to expression in the more intimate processes associated with the activity of the human sense-organs, whose impressions of the world that surrounds us bring about the awakening of our ego-consciousness.

Rudolf Steiner called the Sun 'that has granted us the ego' (ibid.) the second or 'spiritual Sun'. This is a reference to the influence of the seven Sun Elohim. They are the true creators of the human ego, of the 'other self'. Because of this he also called this second Sun the 'ego-engendering Sun' (GA 266/3, 1 June 1913). Finally, the third Sun is Christ Himself or the cosmic Word, which first became the Sun Word or Sun Logos on the Sun and then, on the Earth, the God-man. 'This third Sun has since the Mystery of Golgotha been united with the Earth.[8] The knowledge of this has been guarded by Rosicrucians' (GA 266/3, 18 May 1913).

The Rosicrucians have in their mysteries preserved until our time the secret that 'this spiritual [third] Sun is the Christ principle, which a human individual [since the Mystery of Golgotha] is able to experience within himself once he has understood Paul's words: "Not I, but Christ in me"' (ibid.)[9]; for only Christ as the God of the human ego can endow man with the power of the 'true ego'. This enables him not only to become aware that he is a being who progresses from incarnation to incarnation (this experience is already imparted to him by his experience of the other ego) but also to recognise himself as someone who participates in eternity. Thus it is 'Christ who with His Sun-forces of grace endows us with the higher ego' (ibid.)[10] and makes it possible for us 'to attain eternal life' (ibid.), which in Rosicrucian terminology means to find the divine personality (persona) within oneself.

It follows from this that union with the 'true ego', in accordance with Paul's words: 'Not I, but Christ in me' is the ultimate goal of any ego-development. However, one needs to be aware at this point that the ego which has the capacity to be a chalice for receiving the 'true ego', related as it is to the Being of Christ, is not our ordinary, everyday ego but that 'other ego' which still has to be born in man on the path of modern Christian-Rosicrucian initiation. Thus at the end of the esoteric Lesson from which these quotations have been taken, Rudolf Steiner says: 'It must be the task of every esoteric pupil of the Rose Cross increasingly to understand and bring ever more strongly to consciousness this most spiritual Sun, the Christ'.

The connection of man's threefold ego with the words of Paul can be summarised as follows:

Not I	but Christ	in me
earthly ego	true ego	higher ego

In the sense of modern initiation this 'not I' does not, however, in any way imply the extinguishing of the earthly ego (see further regarding this in chapter 3) but its complete subordination to the higher ego, which must gradually be led to an inner birth within the pupil of the spirit. And once the higher ego has been born within a person as a result of inner development, the Guardian of the Threshold gives the spirit-pupil a further task: 'He has to place what he is in his ordinary self, which appears before him in a picture, under the leadership and guidance of his new-born self' (GA 13, the chapter entitled 'Knowledge of Higher Worlds. Concerning Initiation').

Something similar also subsequently happens with the birth or dawning of the true ego within man, which gradually takes over the leadership role of the higher ego. Once this stage of inner development has been attained, we are already in the presence of a true Christian initiate (Master). 'He stands beyond karma', Rudolf Steiner says of such a person (GA 93a, 24 October 1905). For personal karma is associated with the higher ego, 'which comes to expression in repeated earthly lives' (GA 17, ch.7) and, as we have already seen, has arisen out of the hierarchic order. (Its substance is the sacrificial gift of the Sun Elohim.) This higher ego is pre-eminently the focal point of a human individual's personal karma, which he must himself gradually balance out in the course of his incarnations.

The true ego, on the other hand, which is intimately related to the Logos, is above any personal karma; and so the initiate works only out of the highest necessities of cosmic evolution, as they arise out of the world of Providence. Rudolf Steiner also explains this stage of initiation by saying that being responsible for the beings of karma liberates the Master. He 'is able to renounce the Lipikas' (GA 93a, 24 October 1905). However, this stage can be reached by the initiate only if he is far advanced in the transformation of his physical body into the Spirit Man.[11]

★

The reference to the 'most spiritual Sun', which in the spiritual world is Christ Himself and has always been the object of the quest of all true Rosicrucians (see p. 8), links what has been said above with the Foundation Stone Meditation, at the heart of which there are the radiant tidings of the 'Christ Sun' (fourth part). In its first three parts the three stages of ego-development are also characterised; and they lead towards the [ultimate] aim of man's union with the 'Christ Sun'. Thus in the first microcosmic part of the meditation we have the words:

> Thine own I
> Comes to being
> In the I of God.

This is at the same time a spiritual reflection of the way in which man's higher and true ego are constituted in ordinary life, even though our everyday ego-consciousness has no awareness of these two higher aspects. For it has on Earth no direct connection to the higher ego, which does not descend into the body at incarnation but remains in the spiritual world as in the womb of those divine-spiritual beings whence it originated. This is also the case to an even more heightened degree with the true ego.

If, however, a person imbues his earthly ego with pure thinking and leads it on the path of modern initiation to the reality of the higher ego, the possibility arises for him to permeate it with the Christ substance. This process is characterised in the second microcosmic part:

> Thine own I
> Unite
> With the world I.

Through this ego-related connection with Christ a human individual can rise to an experience of the true ego and thereby enter into a conscious relationship with the entire macrocosm, that is, with the various orders of spiritual hierarchies or divine beings who inhabit it. This occurs just as it is described in the three macrocosmic parts of the meditation, though in a reverse order: from man and the world of elemental spirits that surrounds him through the three groups of three orders of the nine hierarchies to the spirit-sphere of the Trinity itself.

This experience of the true ego is also associated with the highest freedom, whence alone a person can enter consciously into a new, free relationship with the Gods. The consequence of this is that they send him the light of their 'eternal aims', which are constituted in the form of the highest archetype of man as the religion of the Gods.[12]

The words from the third microcosmic part of the Foundation Stone Meditation bear a relationship to this:

> Where the eternal aims of Gods
> World Being's light
> On thine own I
> Bestow
> For thy free willing.

A further dimension to these explorations can be noted through the fact that the first part begins with the reference to the 'world of space', where man develops his ego-consciousness (ordinary ego). In the second part the rhythm of time is referred to. If one interprets these lines as a reference to the esoteric stream of time[13] or to the living time that Christ has brought to humanity from the Sun, it follows that this is also the stream of time in which man's higher ego lives in the spiritual world.[14] And the third part has to do with the 'grounds of eternity' with which man's true ego is primarily associated.

One can also say that the 'free willing' that features in these lines forms the noblest fruit of the development of the earthly ego. 'Thine own I' corresponds to the higher ego, which has already embraced the impulse of freedom; and the 'eternal aims of Gods' become accessible to man through his true ego, since it is from the outset receptive to the 'world being's light' of the spiritual worlds.

The relation between the three aspects of the ego can be clarified by means of the following drawing:

The chalice corresponds here to the 'higher' or 'other' ego, which has the task of bearing and harbouring the 'true ego' in its centre. This ego-chalice is surrounded by a radiating form which is reflected in the bodily sheath and calls forth man's earthly ego-consciousness.[15]

Through thoughts of this nature it becomes more possible to understand the role of the two Guardians of the Threshold in the process of the development of the threefold nature of the human ego. Thus the ordinary ego, when viewed from the threshold of the spiritual world, is related to the human double. When a person advances on the modern path of initiation from the earthly ego to the higher ego, he encounters the lesser Guardian of the Threshold. By following this path from the higher to the true ego, the spirit-pupil encounters the greater Guardian; and when he takes hold of the true ego in Intuition he stands before the cosmic Christ as the cosmic Word, with which as regards its substance the true ego has an essential affinity.

This decisive encounter is preceded by experiences or trials of a highly dramatic nature. Rudolf Steiner refers to them from a more outward aspect in chapter 26 of his autobiography. Here he indicates that, if a human individual is to be able at the threshold to arrive at an experience of his true self, he must at a certain stage of inner development overcome and even extinguish at the abyss of existence everything associated with his earthly ego (which consists mainly of memories of earthly life), without in the process losing his ego-consciousness. This eradication of all memories which connect him with the earthly past can only be accomplished through a *free* resolve of the will. This 'spiritual deed' comes about 'through free inner willing, through an energetic deed of the will' (lecture of 30 August 1913). It can be compared with a real leap across the cosmic abyss. This happens unconsciously with everyone at the moment of going to sleep. 'But it is an entirely different matter in full consciousness to commit one's ego with its memories to annihilation, to forgetfulness, to the abyss, to dwell for a while in the spiritual world at the abyss of existence in the face of utter nothingness. This is the most shattering experience that one can have, and one needs to approach this experience with great trustfulness. In order to approach the abyss as a nothing, one needs to have the trust that the true ego will be brought to one from out of the [super-spiritual] world. And this is indeed what happens ... So the ascent to the super-spiritual world is an inner experience, the experience of a completely new world at the abyss of existence and the receiving of the true ego from this super-spiritual world at the abyss of existence' (ibid.).

The only earthly memory that can accompany a person into the spiritual world at this stage is that of the Mystery of Golgotha, for this is the only earthly event which is at the same time of a supersensible nature. ('It is the only earthly deed that is wholly supersensible', GA 143, 17 December 1912.) If one arrives with such a memory of the Mystery of Golgotha at the threshold of the spiritual world, the Being who meets the person undergoing initiation at the abyss and 'brings' him his true self is Christ Himself. As a result, the initiate who has in this way embraced the true ego is now able to form a conscious connection with the super-spiritual world, which represents the environment for the true ego. (See GA 17, ch. 15.)

However, one must also bear in mind that the memory of the Mystery of Golgotha that is brought here to the threshold of the spiritual world is something altogether different from an ordinary earthly memory. What is involved here is a real search in the spiritual world itself for the essence of Christianity, which consists in the Resurrection of Christ. Hence Rudolf Steiner writes in his auto-biography that at this time he had to 'immerse [himself] in Christianity and, indeed, in the world in which it is illumined from a spiritual standpoint' (GA 28, chapter 26).

In Rudolf Steiner's life this discovery of the innermost essence of

Christianity led him to the culmination of his whole initiation, which he describes as 'having stood in spirit before the Mystery of Golgotha' (ibid.). And as a direct consequence of this he was henceforth able at any time to unite his earthly and his heavenly ego in full consciousness and with complete presence of mind. This was the source of his particular ability to engage in spiritual research at all levels of cosmic existence and present the results of this research in clear and generally comprehensible thoughts in his books and lectures.

The path leading to the attaining of this faculty included a highly dramatic experience,[16] which can only be compared with the brief period in the life of Jesus of Nazareth when, forsaken by the ego of Zarathustra and without as yet having received the Christ into his own being, he was on his way to the Jordan. For when Zarathustra departed from his soul, all the inner forces that had guided him during the 18 years of his presence also immediately forsook him. As he stood at the abyss of nothingness, Jesus now had to employ all his efforts to find his way to the Baptism in the Jordan solely out of that strength which was available to him before his twelfth year, when the ego of Zarathustra had not as yet united with him. He approached the bank of the Jordan filled with the boundless trust that his union with the descending Christ would become possible.

What took place as a world-historical archetype has its direct counterpart in modern initiation in the 'most shattering experience' described above, which the person undergoing initiation is able to withstand in the spiritual world only out of the forces of his 'great trustfulness' with which he 'approaches the abyss as a nothing'. This archetypal trustfulness which Jesus of Nazareth exhibited at the Turning Point of Time on his path to the Jordan is a quality that anyone approaching initiation has since then needed to summon forth at the abyss of existence in order to make the transition from Jesus consciousness to Christ consciousness, which corresponds in modern initiation to the step from the higher to the true ego. Around the turn of the century, this step was one that Rudolf Steiner himself took; and it was out of the Christ consciousness that he thereby attained in the true ego that he was subsequently able to found anthroposophy on the Earth as a modern science of the spirit.

2. The Cosmic Dimension of the Ego

The 'super-spiritual world', where the true ego has its origin, lies above the three worlds with which man is normally connected: the physical world, the soul world and the spiritual world.[17] It follows from this that it is identical with the still higher world which Rudolf Steiner calls the Buddhi plane of the world of Providence.[18] This is the source of the great imagination of the circle of the twelve bodhisattvas who, like twelve stars surrounding the Sun, are gathered around the cosmic Christ. This imagination is one of the central fruits of Rudolf Steiner's research in anthroposophical Christology (see GA 116, 25 October 1909) and gives an indication of the way in which the eventual reconciliation between East and West will come about in future.

On the basis of what has been said, this imagination can be understood as meaning that the twelve bodhisattvas, who, as initiates, have already reached the stage of the higher ego, now in the Buddhi sphere behold the source of the true ego; and from it they receive the forces for their earthly activity.[19] This also corresponds to Rudolf Steiner's indication that six of these bodhisattvas who serve Christ had the task of preparing for His appearance on the Earth, and the other six will ensure that the consequences of the Mystery of Golgotha are brought to humanity (see ibid.).[20]

The archetypal imagination from the Buddhi sphere at the same time makes manifest the inner relationship of the true ego to the higher ego. This is then reflected at the two lower levels, those of the higher ego and the earthly ego. Indeed, in any situation that concerns ego development, the picture immediately arises of a centre surrounded by a twelvefoldness or the imagination of the Sun amidst the twelve constellations.

On the level of the earthly ego, Rudolf Steiner characterises its frame of reference as consisting of twelve different world-conceptions.[21] In the course of his development a person can, on the basis of his earthly ego-consciousness, embrace an ever greater part of these world-conceptions. And when after a series of incarnations he has passed through all twelve points of view, he will—at any rate on the level of thinking—have consciously encompassed the fundamental qualities of his earthly ego. It could even be said that every human ego that accompanies the general cultural development of mankind with sufficient intensity is participating in this process.

A genuine pupil of the spirit (Chela) ascends higher on this path, especially if on the path of his pupilship he has inwardly arrived at the birth of the higher ego. Through this he is able wholly to free himself from his earthly nature and becomes capable of looking upon his ego from outside. As a result it appears to him as divided into a twelvefold form. From the standpoint of the higher ego, he now experiences himself to be standing in the centre surrounded by twelve different pictures of his ego; and just as an earthly human being who has surveyed all twelve world-conceptions fully understands the nature of his earthly ego, so also is it with the higher ego. Anyone who in the spiritual world has been able to imbue all twelve manifestations (pictures) of the ego with his supersensible powers of cognition has to a considerable degree arrived at the essential nature of his higher ego. In other words, just as the sum of the twelve world-conceptions reveals the essence of the earthly ego in its continual process of becoming, so do the twelve manifestations of the ego reveal the essence of man's higher ego.

A similar situation applies in the case of the true ego. Its essential nature is revealed in its true light only when it is reflected back from the surrounding circle of twelve higher egos, as indeed happens in the super-spiritual of Buddhi world. However, because at this spiritual height everything can only consist of beings, the twelve higher egos are represented by the circle of the twelve bodhisattvas. That is, at this juncture there appear the twelve Masters who have inwardly developed the higher ego to the extent that they can in their twelvefold aspect together reveal something of the nature of the true ego and, hence, have the capacity to behold in their midst its cosmic origin and highest source as Christ or the spiritual Sun.

Just as a human being has only 'fathomed his ego in full measure' or 'understood his complete ego'[22] when he has encompassed its twelve manifestations in the spiritual world, so likewise the cosmic nature of Christ can be understood only if one embraces the whole circle of the twelve bodhisattvas or has ascended to the archetypal essence that permeates them all and which Christian esotericism calls the Holy Spirit. (See GA 113, 31 August 1909.) Only when an initiate encompasses this twelvefoldness has he recognised the essential nature of the true ego. Such a Master is then filled with the Holy Spirit and can as a result with his spiritual eyes behold the cosmic Christ amidst the twelve bodhisattvas in His capacity as the source of his true ego.[23]

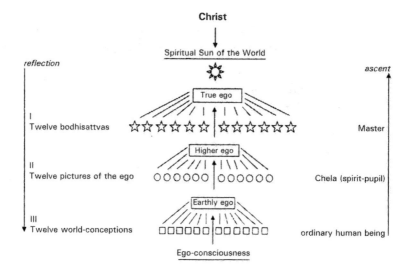

With regard to these three levels of ego-development, it is striking that Rudolf Steiner uses for each of them the image of the Sun in the circle of twelve constellations. This emphasises the fact of the mir-roring process within the various spheres which was referred to earlier. It is only at the lowest level, where there is still a connection with the earthly ego, that the Sun does not appear at the centre of the twelve world-conceptions but stands in the midst of the seven planets. (See GA 151, 22 January 1914.) At the middle level, which is related to the higher ego, the human ego does indeed begin to work out of the power of the Sun; but it cannot as yet penetrate to the Sun's essential being, which is why Rudolf Steiner is still using the image of the Sun here as a comparison. (See GA 119, 29 March 1910.) Only at the highest level, which is associated with the true ego, does the Christ Sun Himself appear, in order to fill the twelve bodhisattvas with the divine *life* that becomes cosmic wisdom within them. Hence only after the last of the twelve has fulfilled his mission on the Earth will human beings be able truly to recognise Christ in His full cosmic significance.

What comes to manifestation here is a cosmic archetype which is mirrored on the two lower levels. Rudolf Steiner also describes it in the following words: 'We have now ascended into the sphere of the bodhisattvas and entered a circle of twelve stars, in the midst of which is the Sun, illuminating and warming them; and from this Sun they derive the source of life which it is their task to bring down to the Earth' (GA 116, 25 October 1909). From this and similar descriptions it is clear that Rudolf Steiner had himself reached the corresponding stage of modern initiation, in order that he might subsequently be able to communicate these fruits of his spiritual research to others.

As has already been shown, these three aspects of human individuality correspond in their cosmic aspect to the mystery of the threefold Sun and in their human aspect to the three stages of man's spiritual development. Especially in some early lectures Rudolf Steiner characterises these stages as follows: a person who is at the highest level of cultural development in his time (or is even a genius), then a Chela or spirit-pupil and finally a Master. (See GA 94, 28 October 1906.) The former works upon the acquiring and interconnecting of all twelve world-conceptions, the harmonious interplay of which embraces the whole of human culture. The second seeks to bring about the spiritual synthesis of all twelve images of his ego that he encounters in the spiritual world; and the Master ascends to the point of taking hold of his true ego in order by means of its forces to experience Christ in the Buddhi sphere.[24]

A further aspect of the relationship of the higher ego to the true ego must also be mentioned here. Even if the spirit-pupil has not yet fully reached the stage of the higher ego, it is possible for him to gain an initial experience of it through a true spiritual Master. Thus Rudolf Steiner says: 'Man's higher self is not something that lives within him but is around him. *The higher self consists of more highly evolved indi-*

vidualities. A person must be clear about the fact that the higher self is outside him. If he were to seek it within himself, he would never find it. He must seek it through those [individualities of the Masters] who have already travelled the [spiritual] path that we wish to follow' (GA 93a, 18 October 1905).

Moreover, because such exalted Masters themselves already bear within themselves the true ego, they can significantly shorten and relieve the burden of the path which the spirit-pupils who seek an inner access to them need to follow to their higher ego; for in accordance with the law of the spiritual world, the development of a lower bodily member can only be brought about and accelerated by a higher one.[25]

Among the Masters who are particularly suited to guide the pupil of the spirit on the modern path of initiation to an inner experience of the higher ego, Rudolf Steiner especially mentions Manes, Zarathustra (Master Jesus) and Scythianos, whom he calls the 'great revered bodhisattvas of the West' (GA 113, 31 August 1909). And it is clear from the further indication that these Masters were from the outset 'the teachers in the schools of the Rose Cross' (ibid.) that also the highest leader and founder of these esoteric schools through which 'all the wisdom of the bodhisattvas of the post-Atlantean period was to flow ever more strongly into the future evolution of mankind' (ibid.)—namely, Christian Rosenkreutz himself—is also such a Master. The modern spirit-pupil can receive the strongest impulses for the development of his higher ego not only from these four Masters but also from Rudolf Steiner, who since his last incarnation has belonged to this circle of the leading Rosicrucian Masters[26] and who today likewise works as the great inspirer of the higher ego and as the one who furthers its development amongst mankind.

And above this lodge of the exalted Christian Masters, as the spiritual Sun of the 'Master of Masters' who pervades and unifies them all, is Christ Himself, the divine centre of the bodhisattva sphere in the world of Providence. From this region, where the initiate finds a fully conscious connection with his true ego, ever new impulses may be drawn down for the higher ego in order that from this source the earthly ego of human beings can be fructified and guided on the path of its further evolution (see chapter 3).

★

The interaction between all three aspects of the ego can also be viewed in terms of the form of the cross. Its horizontal dimension corresponds to the evolution of the higher ego or the human *individuality* which passes through all earthly incarnations. It begins with A (the first incarnation) and reaches its goal with Ω (the last incarnation). This evolution is referred to by Christ when He says: 'I am the A and the Ω, the beginning and the end' (Rev. 1:8).

The vertical dimension indicates the genesis of the human *personality*. It forms a kind of axis or column which has the task of uniting heaven and Earth in a new, inseparable unity.[27] The base of this column corresponds to the earthly ego or man's earthly personality, in which alone full self-consciousness and, hence, true freedom can be attained upon the foundation of the physical body; whereas the uppermost part of the column corresponds to the true ego, which brings the eternal persona to manifestation in the heights of the spiritual world. Rudolf Steiner says: 'An experience of oneself in the true ego comes about approximately at the mid-point between death and a new birth' (GA 147, 31 August 1913), that is, only at the spiritual height of the cosmic midnight hour, when a human being encounters the future purpose of the evolution that he experiences as an eternal persona out of the power of the true ego.

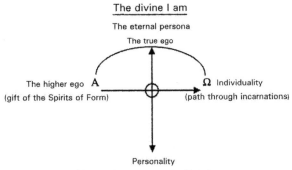

As is apparent from the content of this book, the conscious relationship between the true ego or a human individual's eternal persona and his earthly ego was established for the first time through Christ's appearance on the Earth; and it was through the Mystery of Golgotha that the possibility arose for every human being who connects himself with the Christ impulse to unite earthly ego-consciousness as the bearer of human autonomy and freedom with the true ego. Thus the following of this path that leads from the earthly ego to the true ego is possible only if a person has previously united himself with his higher ego (see the point of intersection in the drawing). On Christ's path from the spiritual heights to the Earth, this point corresponds to His union with the Sun.

On the pre-Christian path of initiation it was pre-eminently Krishna who led his pupils to an experience of the higher ego. Hence Rudolf Steiner says: 'When someone looks up to Krishna, he is at the same time looking up to his own highest self' (GA 142, 30 December 1912). Since the Mystery of Golgotha, when the decisive step from the individuality to the personality was inaugurated, this path has fundamentally changed. Since then, what Rudolf Steiner describes in the following words has acquired validity: ' "I" is the word of Krishna; "Not I, but Christ in me" are the words of the Christ impulse' (GA 146, 5 June 1913). For only in the sense of this second dictum is man's connection forged with the true ego and, hence, with the eternal persona which is the aim of his whole evolution.

In this sense the words of Paul can be related in an altogether different way to the three aspects of the human ego than was the case in the first chapter. We now have the following picture:

Not I,	but Christ	in me
higher ego	true ego	earthly ego
(Krishna)		

For after the Baptism in the Jordan, when the higher ego (of Zarathustra) had already left the sheaths of Jesus of Nazareth, the true ego was through the Christ Himself directly able to form a connection within him with the earthly ego.[28]

In this way there is a mystery of the greatest profundity associated with the human ego which can never be fully fathomed. The following mysterious words in *Theosophy* refer to this: 'The "seer" can behold the influence of the ego upon the aura. The "ego" itself is invisible even to him; it truly resides within the "veiled holy of holies of man's being"' (GA 9).

★

The relationship of the ego to the three spiritual members of man's being, especially to Manes or the Spirit Self, represents a further mystery. The most familiar definition that Rudolf Steiner gave in this regard is that the Spirit Self represents the astral body which has been fully spiritualised by the ego. (Similarly, the Life Spirit and the Spirit Man are, respectively, ether and physical bodies that have been transformed by the ego.)

There is another description of the Spirit Self which is similarly given in *Theosophy*: 'The spirit irradiates the ego and lives within it as in its sheath, just as the ego dwells in the body and the soul as its sheaths. The spirit forms the ego from within outwards, the mineral world from without inwards. The spirit that forms an ego and lives as the ego may be called the "Spirit Self", because it manifests itself as the "I", or ego or self, of man' (GA 9, 'The Nature of Man: Body, Soul and Spirit'). What is striking about these words is that the ego referred to here is clearly a combination of earthly ego and higher ego; for the mineral world forms the earthly ego from without inwards, whereas the spirit forms the higher ego from within outwards. This characterises the situation in human evolution which arises after the birth of the higher ego in the earthly ego and therefore forms a bridge for taking hold of the Spirit Self.

The process whereby the spirit, coming from the higher worlds, fashions the human ego from within and develops it further can be experienced only by the awakened higher ego.[29] But this process can take place only if the astral body has been purified and spiritualised to a certain extent by the person concerned. Otherwise this work of the spirit on his ego will not be carried out in the right way. If one views these two processes together, one has defined the true nature of the Spirit Self. Indeed, both happen simultaneously; for on the one hand there is the result of the transforming work of the ego on the astral body and, on the other, the presence of the spirit in the human ego that has been made possible through this work. And then through his higher ego the human individual can consciously engage in this twofold development of the Spirit Self within his being.

In this regard, the following passage from the cycle on the Gospel of St. John, where Rudolf Steiner speaks about the wedding at Cana in connection with the sixth epoch and, in so doing, characterises the relationship between the higher self and Manas, acquires a particular significance: 'This sixth cultural epoch will be of great importance ... [It will be a time when] the higher self will, for the part of mankind that is at a normal level of development, descend *initially in its lower form as the Spirit Self or Manas*. A connection of the human ego—in the way that it has gradually been developed—with the unifying qualities of the higher ego will then take place. We can call this a spiritual marriage; and this is what the connection of the human ego with Manas or the Spirit Self has always been called in Christian esotericism' (GA 103, 30 May 1908—I). And in an earlier lecture Rudolf Steiner links the mystery of this inner work of the awakened higher ego on the development of the three spiritual members of man's being with the most intimate and holiest tasks of true Rosicrucians: 'Atma-Buddhi-Manas, the higher self, is the mystery that will become manifest when the sixth sub-race will be sufficiently mature for this. Christian Rosenkreutz will then no longer need to be there in a warning capacity, but everything that has signified battle on the outward plane will find peace through the Molten Sea, through the holy Golden Triangle' (GA 93, 4 November 1904). Here the Golden Triangle refers to the threefoldness of Manas-Buddhi-Atma; and the Molten Sea is what a person must engender inwardly in order to awaken the higher ego,[30] as indicated in the trial by fire which Hiram undergoes.[31]

In this way Rudolf Steiner connects the essence of St. John's Gospel with Hiram's experience of the mysteries and, hence, with the esoteric stream of Christian Rosenkreutz, who through his initiation in the thirteenth century attained the stage of the true ego.[32]

From both quotations (but especially from the first) it is unmistakably clear that the spiritual members of man's being correspond to the three ascending stages of ego-development, and that in the sixth cultural epoch the right connection with the Spirit Self can be made only on the foundation of an awakened higher ego. Otherwise, the union with it will have a distinctly luciferic character, a danger to which Rudolf Steiner has expressly referred.[33]

Whereas the higher ego has, as regards the receiving of the spiritual members, more the task in the coming cultural epochs of a conscious supervision of this process and only a small possibility of active engagement in it, it will in the course of its full development in future planetary stages of our cosmos play an active and creative part. For the ultimate transformation of the astral body into the Spirit Self on the future Jupiter can take place only out of the forces of the fully developed higher ego, which for a creative activity of this nature must have attained a conscious connection with Christ on the level of the true ego. The same also applies to the transformation of the ether body into the Life Spirit on Venus and, moreover, to the transformation of the physical body into the Spirit Man on Vulcan.

This evolution, in which ego-development forms a continuous axis, can be discerned most clearly by means of a kind of Caduceus sign (Mercury staff):

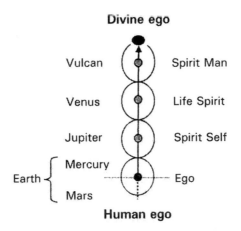

It must be emphasised here that the connection with the Manas forces in the sixth cultural epoch will be of a completely different character from the situation pertaining on the future Jupiter. In the former case there will be an outpouring of Manas into man through a kind of higher revelation from spiritual heights, while in the latter case it will be taken hold of by the full power of the human ego. Hence Rudolf Steiner says: 'On Jupiter man will relate to the Spirit Self somewhat in the way that he relates on Earth to the ego' (GA 130, 9 January 1912). If we view what has been said in the context of the first definition of the Spirit Self as an astral body that has been fully transformed by the ego, we can characterise the whole process as follows. On the future Jupiter the astral body, as Manas (Spirit Self), will be imbued with the power of the individual ego to the full extent of its substance and will therefore be a precise reflection of the ego. The same will happen on the future Venus with the ether body. In its transmuted form it will, as Life Spirit, likewise be imbued in its every part by the power of the ego. And on Vulcan the same metamorphosis will also take hold of the physical body. Its supersensible form will then have a conscious ego-character in all its various aspects, as a result of which the ego will have attained the highest stage of its evolution. 'Our ego is the infant member of our human nature, it is the youngest. This ego will be formed in the way that the physical body is now only on Vulcan [that is, it will similarly reach the fourth stage, just as the physical body has reached it in our time in its evolution from Old Saturn] ... But this ego resides at the same time in the womb of the spiritual world' (GA 157a, 20 November 1915). That it is the higher ego with which we are concerned here is clear from another lecture, where this ego which dwells in the spiritual world without descending to earthly incarnations is described as deriving from the Spirits of Form. 'The ego remains there, it remains fundamentally in the form in which, as we know, it has been bestowed on us by the Spirits of Form. This ego is retained in the spiritual world' (GA 165, 19 December 1915).

In another passage Rudolf Steiner likewise attests that the human ego will reach its ultimate fulfilment only on Vulcan. 'On the last earthly incarnation of Vulcan, the ego will have reached the highest point of its evolution' (GA 99, 31 May 1907). This will come about when the ego has endowed the whole of the physical body to the ultimate degree with an ego quality. What this actually means was demonstrated in terms of spiritual history through the Resurrection of

Christ, when for the first time an earthly body came into being which reflected the Ego of Christ in absolute perfection and could therefore exist in equal measure in the physical and spiritual worlds. Hence Rudolf Steiner says: 'There [in the Mystery of Golgotha] we have the being as a God that man will be as a human being at the end of Vulcan evolution' (GA 346, 7 September 1924). For this reason, the seventh—spiritual—member of man's being is called the *Spirit Man*; for it is a being who, as man, has become spirit to the full extent of his physical body. And the path towards the attainment of this goal has been opened up to all earthly human beings through the Resurrection of Christ.

At this point the following thoughts may be added. In the course of his description of man's pilgrimage through the spirit-land after death in his book *Theosophy*, Rudolf Steiner refers to a significant difference between the Spirit Self, on the one hand, and the two higher spiritual members of the Life Spirit and Spirit Man, on the other.

The Spirit Self has its home or its origin in Higher Devachan—or, to be precise, from the fifth region upwards. Rudolf Steiner writes about this as follows: 'We see, therefore, that what in this book has been called the Spirit Self lives, in this [fifth] region—in so far as it is developed—in the reality that is appropriate to it' ('The Three Worlds: The Spirit in the Spirit-land after Death'). This sentence follows immediately after the indication that at this stage a person has an experience of his former incarnations and also a prophetic vision of all of his subsequent ones. This knowledge does, however, belong to the nature of the higher ego; and its relationship to the Spirit Self in man's life after death arises from this situation.

The two higher spiritual members—the Life Spirit and Spirit Man—have a completely different source; for they derive not from Higher Devachan but from the region lying above it, which therefore extends beyond the 'three worlds' described in *Theosophy*. Thus in the chapter 'The Spirit-land' Rudolf Steiner writes that at the upper limit of 'the three worlds' a person arrives at an experience of the 'life kernels' which, while indeed manifesting their influence in Higher Devachan, nevertheless essentially belong to a still higher world. Man is himself the bearer of such a life kernel, which has its origin in still higher regions. Rudolf Steiner says regarding this life kernel: 'When man was [previously] described according to the parts out of which he is constituted, this life kernel was specifically associated with him and the "Life Spirit" and "Spirit Man" were cited as belonging to it'.

From the words that have been quoted, it becomes apparent that these two spiritual members have an inner relationship to man's true ego, which can likewise live and manifest its activity on Higher Devachan (the super-spiritual world) but, as regards its essential nature, originates not from there but from still higher spheres. This can also be expressed by saying that the higher ego finds its fulfilment in man's work in bringing the Spirit Self into being, just as the true ego is active in the development of the Spirit Man.[34] And the Life Spirit forms the living bridge or the transition between them.

In Rosicrucian esotericism, this process of transforming the lower members into higher ones was always called the building of the inner temple. This is what Rudolf Steiner is referring to when he says: 'What is now in its early stages, the "baby" within man's being, is the ego. This is fourfold man who has the ego dwelling within him, as the temple containing the statue of a God' (GA 93a, 7 October 1905). Out of fourfold man, whose crowning element is the earthly ego as the bearer of freedom, the temple for the higher ego is built into which it subsequently moves as a divine statue. This higher ego is then, like the magic lamp from Goethe's Fairy Tale, able to transform the temple from within: the astral body into the Spirit Self, the ether body into the Life Spirit and the physical body into the Spirit Man. Earthly man will in this way gradually become cosmic man. If viewed from the standpoint of the evolution of the higher ego, these three transformations correspond to the cognitive stages of Imagination, Inspiration and Intuition.

Man can begin and implement this process only on the Earth, out of his earthly ego; for in it alone can human freedom be experienced as an essential condition of the whole path and, hence, incorporated into the further development of the higher self. 'This is he who has developed his higher self. The physical world is where this development takes place' (GA 94, 5 March 1906). However, this ultimate goal can be attained only through a conscious relationship with the true ego (see the diagram on p. 19), which alone makes it possible for the forces of the ego to reach their full maturity and work right into the physical body.

The first stage of this process is, as already indicated, the work of the ego on the astral body, which gives rise to Manas. Once this work within man's being has advanced to the point where his ego has to a great extent formed its connection with Manas, Rudolf Steiner uses both terms synonymously. Especially in early lectures he employs the two names in this way: 'Manas is the fifth principle, the spiritual principle in man, which is to arise and to which a temple was to be erected' (GA 93, 22 May 1905). And in a lecture from the following year he says: 'If one conceives of the cosmic intelligence as the world of thoughts that are accessible to the higher ego (Manas) ...';[35] or, somewhat later on in the same lecture: 'One may continue to imagine the power of the higher ego, of Manas, within man ...' (GA 94, 9 June 1906).[36] Moreover, Rudolf Steiner frequently describes the connection with the higher self with words that almost exactly reflect man's union with the Spirit Self in the sixth cultural epoch. In both cases there is an outpouring of higher spiritual forces from above into man's essential being. 'The inner aspect [of man's being] must be made receptive to the absorption of the higher self. If it is indeed receptive, man's higher self will then stream into human nature' (GA 103, 31 May 1908). Human individuals must prepare themselves for this inner receptiveness through a conscious purification of their astral body out of the forces of their earthly ego.

The most striking example of such an equivalence of the concepts of 'Manas' and 'higher ego' arises if one considers this process from the standpoint of the activity of Angels. Thus Rudolf Steiner says the following with regard to the encounter that a person has at night with his Angel: 'And whether one says that someone is looking up to his higher self, which he is supposed to come increasingly to resemble, or that he is looking up to his Angel as his great model is actually from a spiritual point of view the same thing' (GA 105, 6 August 1908). Rudolf Steiner had already referred to such a relationship of man's higher ego to the beings of the spiritual world in *Knowledge of the*

Higher Worlds, although in this book intended for the wider public it is formulated in a more general way: 'He [the spirit-pupil] learns to know how his higher self is connected with lofty spiritual beings and *forms a unity with them*' (GA 10, 'Some Effects of Initiation'). It is significant that in a later lecture on 20 February 1917 Rudolf Steiner says virtually the same thing about the relationship of the Spirit Self to a person's Angel.

Rudolf Steiner also adds a human aspect to this perspective from the sphere of the Angels. The growing awareness of the higher ego is, as we have already seen, brought into connection with the nature and influence of the initiates who guide the evolution of humanity: 'What our self will be in several thousand years is now our higher self. But in order to become properly acquainted with the higher self, we must look for it where it already lives today, namely in higher indivi- dualities. This is a matter of pupils associating with the Masters' (GA 93a, 18 October 1905). The reference to 'several thousand years' points initially to the sixth cultural epoch, when mankind will receive the forces of the Spirit Self from the spiritual world; and if human individuals prepare themselves rightly in our time for this future, they will also be able to experience the nature of their individuality in a new form in the epoch of the Spirit Self. 'And through the very fact that people experience this ego merely as a reflection in the course of our fifth post-Atlantean cultural period, they are being made ready to experience the ego *in a new form* in the sixth epoch. It is characteristic of this age of the consciousness soul that man receives his ego only in the form of a reflection, so that as he familiarises himself with the age of the Spirit Self he is able to experience the ego differently, *in a new form*' (GA 187, 27 December 1918).

It is through this experience of the ego as a reflection in the fifth post-Atlantean cultural epoch that it is possible to develop one's ego- consciousness to its full capacity and, hence, arrive at inner freedom. This ego-conscious freedom can then be assimilated within one's higher ego and in the sixth epoch united with the Spirit Self that streams down from above. Through this one acquires a conscious access to the forces of the spirit, in a manner that accords with the second definition of the Spirit Self in *Theosophy* (see page 21). This means that the spirit that originates from supersensible worlds and forms the ego from within will come increasingly to manifestation as the forces of the Spirit Self descend, with the result that the ego attains ever higher stages of its consciousness in the spiritual world. Hence Rudolf Steiner says that the sixth cultural epoch will be a clairvoyant epoch, when all human beings who are at the general level of cultural development will possess the faculty of beholding the spiritual world with full consciousness. (See GA 13.)

This faculty which will be generally disseminated amongst mankind in the sixth cultural epoch can be attained already today on the anthroposophical path of schooling. In order to have a better understanding of this path, one needs to bear in mind that in our time the whole of present-day culture is constantly preoccupied not only with individual ego-development but also with the purifying of the astral body through the impulses of the ego and, hence, with its gradual transformation into the Spirit Self. 'In general we can say of people today that they use their experiences for transforming their astral bodies ... Now what is wholly consciously developed by the ego within the astral body is called the Spirit Self or Manas' (GA 94, 28 October 1906).[37]

What in this way is currently happening through the overall cultural evolution of humanity cannot as yet be extended on the same level of development to the two higher spiritual members (Buddhi and Atma). For 'modern man lives in a Manas condition, that is, he can indeed make significant changes in his astral body but not as yet in his ether body and least of all in his physical body' (ibid.). The reason for this is that inner work on the spiritual transformation of these two members of man's being is only possible out of an awakened higher ego. Hence Rudolf Steiner says: 'Through the work of *our higher ego* we transform the perishable bodies that have been given to us by the Gods and fashion eternal bodies for ourselves' (GA 93a, 24 October 1905). But such esoteric work with respect to the Spirit Self must begin even now; for what has developed hitherto within human nature as a whole will no longer suffice for the future. Thus the transformation of the astral body into the Spirit Self needs to take place in our time on two levels: on the one hand out of the forces of the earthly ego for all human beings sharing in overall cultural development and, on the other hand, out of the forces of the higher ego on the part of those people who want to prepare for the imminent sixth cultural epoch on the modern path of schooling. This inner work can also be termed the path that leads towards the Spirit Self. In this way the fifth and sixth epochs have a common task. Hence Rudolf Steiner emphasises in *Occult Science* that 'the fifth and sixth periods ... are in a certain sense the decisive ones' (GA 13, 'Present and Future Evolution of the World and of Mankind'). While in *Theosophy* this is referred to with the words: 'Consciousness and Spirit Self form a unity' (GA 9, 'The Nature of Man: Body, Soul and Spirit'). This unity, however, arises through a person's endeavours to unite his consciousness soul with the spirit out of the ego, so that it becomes a 'spirit-filled consciousness soul' (ibid.). This process of spiritualisation begins already with the first stage of the modern path of schooling, which Rudolf Steiner refers to as that of the study of what has been imparted through spiritual science (see GA 13).

In the sixth cultural epoch, the Manas in those individuals who have been prepared for this through esoteric development in the fifth epoch will have the capacity to receive the outpouring of Buddhi forces from above. 'In the sixth cultural period, the Spirit Self that has [in the fifth epoch] evolved from the consciousness soul will unite with the Life Spirit ... In this sixth age there will then be a celebration of the great marriage of humanity where the Spirit Self unites with the Life Spirit' (GA 100, 25 November 1907). There is a prophetic indication of this in St. John's Gospel in the form of the wedding at Cana (ibid.). This represents the marriage of the forces of Christ and Sophia, which corresponds to the union of Buddhi and Manas within man; and this union will reach its culmination in the sixth epoch and will pervade the whole cultural development of humanity, as Novalis has already prophetically discerned.[38]

The outpouring of Buddhi forces will then occur for human beings not in the way that natural clairvoyance formerly shone forth but as a kind of spontaneous initiation, which will as a consequence bring about a deeper and more conscious connection with the spiritual world. For 'the moment when Buddhi is engendered is in all mysteries called a second birth, new birth or awakening' (GA 94, 28 October 1906).[39] This 'new birth' in the spirit will then give rise to the true flowering of ego-consciousness within man which will take place in the sixth epoch. If we again recall that Christ first and foremost brought the Buddhi forces to the Earth, we will also rightly understand the following words: 'Christ appears in order to give to mankind forces that can enable the highest ego-consciousness to be attained in the sixth age' (GA 100, 25 November 1907).

The awakening of Lazarus at the Turning Point of Time and of Christian Rosenkreutz in the middle of the thirteenth century represent a kind of archetype for such 'new births'. Hence the Rose Cross will 'be the symbol of the new Christianity of the sixth sub-race' (GA 93, 4 November 1904), the Christianity of Christ and Sophia which is being prepared already in our time within anthroposophy. 'Those who are today inwardly preparing themselves for the development of the Spirit Self will in the next age [out of the Buddhi forces] make this deeper, spiritual Christianity ever more accessible to mankind' (GA 100, 21 November 1907).

In our time only a highly evolved spirit-pupil is able to reach this stage in the course of a real initiation. For 'a Chela proceeds directly to spiritualise everything even to the extent of his ether body. Chelahood is accomplished when he has enabled Buddhi to stream fully into his life body, so that the life body that has been ennobled by the [higher] ego becomes the Life Spirit' (GA 94, 28 October 1906). Still higher lies the stage of a 'Master', who already within Earth evolution has to a certain extent transformed his physical body into the Spirit Man, thereby achieving the ideal of the seventh cultural epoch. Such a Master has even been elevated above the principle of karma. (See p. 8.) In these spiritual heights he is able to take upon himself the karma of other people, which then affects him right into his physical body.

This is what Rudolf Steiner accomplished at the Christmas Conference through the refounding of the Anthroposophical Society, when he voluntarily united even his own karma with it and thereby embarked on his sacrificial path as a modern imitator of Christ. And the spiritual world, in fully affirming his deed, accordingly endowed him with the loftiest revelations of karma and with the founding of the School of Michael on the Earth.[40]

★

To conclude this chapter, there is a further aspect of the way that the three aspects of human individuality work within man that needs to be considered. As has already been indicated, the seven Elohim implanted the true ego out of the sphere of the Logos into the higher ego that had been created by them in Lemuria. Since then it has formed the innermost core of the human ego. This process was not one that human beings could consciously experience, for they had to wait a long time until the possibility was given to them through the Mystery of Golgotha of fully taking hold of their ego. Only after this was man able to say with respect to Christ: 'Christ gives me my significance' (GA 127, 25 February 1911); for, as has already been said, it has only been possible for man's earthly ego to have a relationship to his true ego as a result of the Mystery of Golgotha. This occurred through Christ's union with the earthly ego of Jesus of Nazareth at the Turning Point of Time. Until then the spiritual hierarchies had to nurture this relationship. Even today this can be discerned in the development of a child until the awakening of its ego in its third year. Rudolf Steiner says in this connection: 'If we have before us a little child [up to the age of three and a half] and contemplate it clairvoyantly, we are aware of its ego in the form of an aura, but radiant energies flow from this aura of the ego to the higher hierarchies, to the Angels, Archangels and so forth, and the forces of the hierarchies stream into it' (ibid.).

Rudolf Steiner describes the influence of the beings of the Third Hierarchy in the little child elsewhere in connection with the three qualities that are developed at this age in every person: upright posture, speaking and thinking. Thus Rudolf Steiner speaks of how the Archai endow the child from the spiritual world with the capacity of walking, the Archangels with that of speaking and the Angels with that of thinking. (See GA 226, 18 May 1923.)

Both in the lecture quoted above and in the book *The Spiritual Guidance of the Individual and Humanity* (GA 15, chapter 1), Rudolf Steiner associates this threefold gift from the spiritual world to the child with the influence of Christ, as He had worked into human evolution from earliest times from outside the Earth and specifically from the Sun. In addition to what is described in the book referred to above, it can also be said that Christ works here through the true ego within man; and His influence is mediated with respect to the various qualities of the three faculties by the corresponding beings of the Third Hierarchy. This influence also continues to exist in a person's later life, albeit in a different form. He is just as unaware of this in his ego-consciousness (in his earthly ego) as he generally is of the influence of his true ego in ordinary life; for an experience of this nature lies no less deeply beneath the surface of waking consciousness as do the spiritual forces of earliest childhood.

If we now endeavour to understand this process from the standpoint of human evolution, we arrive at the following overall perspective. In the Lemurian age the seven Sun Elohim as leading Spirits of Form endowed man from the Sun with the substance of the ego and implanted into it the spark of the Logos, the true ego. This event was a deeply unconscious process for mankind at that time; and it was the Elohim themselves who had to establish the mediating link between the true ego and man's actual ego (the higher ego). After the Fall, when the direct relationship of human beings to the Sun sphere of the Elohim was increasingly severed, the spirits of the Third Hierarchy took over this task. At the same time they gradually brought to an evolving humanity the three gifts that were mentioned above, which a human individual receives even today in his earliest childhood.

Thus in the later periods of Lemuria (after the Fall) it was above all the Archai who established the relationship within man to the true ego. At the same time he was through this relationship also endowed with the ability to walk with an upright posture. On Atlantis the Archangels in particular had the task of watching over the relationship of the true ego to man and also bestowed on him the faculty of speech.

In the post-Atlantean age the same task was undertaken by the Angels with regard to the awakening faculty of thinking. They were now in a position to bring about man's relationship to his true ego, of which he continued to have no notion in his earthly consciousness.

That this guidance by the Angels in the post-Atlantean age con-

tinued until the Turning Point of Time is attested by the figure of John
the Baptist, whose influence is referred to at the beginning of the
Gospel of St. Mark: 'See, I send my Angel before you; he is to prepare
your way' (1:2; translation by Jon Madsen). This is an indication that at
this time the connection of the true ego with man was ensured only
through the mediation of the Angel.[41] And because an angelic being
was working particularly strongly in John, he was able to sense the
influence of the forces of his true ego (even though as yet unconsciously). He was through this prepared and predestined in a way that
no other person was at that time to recognise Christ on the Earth and
to guide other human beings to Him.

John's central demand: 'Change your hearts and minds. The realm
of the heavens has come close' (Matthew 3:2, translation by Jon
Madsen) also confirms this. The words 'hearts and minds' (or 'inner
orientation') here refer mainly to the faculty of thinking, which in the
case of John was—through the mediation of the Angel—able to work
as the revelation of his true ego. Rudolf Steiner describes this in the
following words: 'In John there lives an angelic being who takes
possession of his soul, a being who leads human beings to Christ [and
at the same time to the embracing of the true ego]. He is a sheath for
the revelation of this angelic being' (GA 127, 25 February 1911).

What had still lived within the Baptist as an influence deriving from
beyond the human world that sought to maintain the connection with
the true ego was fundamentally changed as a result of Christ's
appearance on the Earth. Since then a human individual can establish a
direct connection between his earthly ego and the true ego, and
consciously take hold of the latter, only through his relationship to
Christ.

Rudolf Steiner describes this decisive transformation in the evolution of mankind inaugurated by the Mystery of Golgotha as follows:
'In pre-Christian times the angelic beings exercised their influence
over man, because he did not as yet have the ego *as an earthly ideal.*[42]
Since human beings have had the light of the Sun of Christ they have
been able to direct their countenance to Him, with the result that they
are imbued with a power formerly bestowed upon them by the
Angels. So whereas he formerly received the inspirations of the Angels

[and still earlier those of the Archangels and Archai], man must in our time receive the Christ through his devotion to the Christ Being' (ibid.). And then immediately afterwards he refers to the words of Paul through which he connects the whole process with the new Christian mysteries that have as their focal point the encompassing of the true ego by man's ego-consciousness. 'Whereas John was able to say: "Not I, but the Angel within me has come as an emissary", people in our time must say, as did Paul: "Not I, but Christ in me".' And then Rudolf Steiner adds: 'They should learn to understand Christ in the light of the teachings of spiritual science' (ibid.).

He then goes on to describe the whole process from the point of view of the influence of Christ within the child: 'The essential quality of being imbued with Christ, of fulfilling the words of St. Paul "Christ in me", becomes a reality when we say that we must devote the whole of our life to what lives within us during our earliest childhood; for then Christ is indeed within us' (ibid.). And according to Rudolf Steiner, this is how spiritual science would understand the ultimate purpose of earthly evolution: 'When earthly evolution has come to an end and we have passed through our many incarnations, we shall need to have *consciously* imbued ourselves with what lived unconsciously within us in our earliest childhood' (ibid.). In other words: the earthly ego must consciously embrace the true ego within man's higher ego, which passes through all incarnations and forges them within itself into a higher unity, and thereby engender within itself the new Christ consciousness. The task of the new Christian mysteries is to lead human beings to this goal.

Rudolf Steiner refers to this in connection with the words of John the Baptist that have already been quoted, which in our time must be understood completely differently in the light of the new mysteries. 'Let us try to cultivate the thought that the words: "Change your inner orientation, for the time is at hand" apply as much to our time as they did to the time of Christ. Whereas at that time [at the Turning Point of Time] they meant that "the realm of the heavens has come close", we must today look prophetically into the near future and say: "for the human ego is near to the kingdom of heaven"' (GA 125, 23 January 1910). And immediately after these words he adds: 'Let us prepare ourselves through a faithful study of spiritual science for making ourselves worthy to enter [as an ego] into the kingdom that awaits our response. And we ourselves can only grow in stature if we [as an ego-being] find the path to the kingdom of heaven' (ibid.).

On this path, too, an ultimate synthesis between the individual and social elements of humanity can be achieved. For the source of all differences between human beings is that the higher ego, which at the beginning of earthly evolution consisted for all human individuals of an empty vessel, has over the course of incarnations gradually become full of quite different elements (a variety of earthly experiences). The result of this is that the reflection of this ego in the human body, which is to say the earthly ego, is experienced in a completely individual way (i.e. differently) by every human being. In contrast, their true egos are—because of their primal and substantial connection with the Logos—not separated from one another but are united with one another in Christ. They together represent the individual members of the cosmic Ego-being of Christ, in which the individual and the social are no longer at variance with one another but have both reached their fullest development. Rudolf Steiner speaks in the following words about this twofold influence of Christ with respect to man: 'The Christ impulse has access to human individuality, and it must be active in the innermost depths of human nature if it is to become effective. It is not the forces of the intellect but the deepest forces of man's heart and soul which need to receive the Christ impulse; but once it has been received this impulse works not in furtherance of the individual aspect of human nature but of its universal aspect' (GA 240, 25 January 1924). This is the unique quality of Christ consciousness within man, where all polarities unite in a higher synthesis.

In this way man attains in the new mysteries a conscious relationship to his true ego, in which alone Christ can be fully and consciously experienced without ego-consciousness (the earthly ego) being in the smallest way impeded.

This is the unique quality of the Christ impulse, which was inaccessible to the whole of pre-Christian evolution and therefore had to be replaced by the collective work of the Third Hierarchy. In our time, however, every human individual can, as an ego-being who has reached the age of majority, himself take hold of the destiny of his ego, in order through the new relationship to Christ to lead the ego to the ultimate purpose of its evolution, which is at the same time the ultimate purpose of the Earth.

3. The Significance of the Earthly Ego

'The reason for the Earth's existence is to give man full self-consciousness, the "I am".'

Rudolf Steiner

'Human ego-consciousness was to be purified and sanctified by Christianity.'

Rudolf Steiner[43]

From what has been said so far, the reader may well have the impression that, in comparison to the higher—and still more to the true—ego, man's earthly ego, or to be more precise the ego-consciousness associated with it, should be valued less than the two other aspects of human individuality. However, this is not the case. For since the Mystery of Golgotha, it is precisely this earthly ego of man that has acquired a central significance for the whole future of human evolution. This happened after Christ had lived for three years on the Earth in the earthly ego of Jesus of Nazareth and had completely transformed it in the Mystery of Golgotha. In order to come closer to an answer to the question as to how things stand with man's earthly ego, it is necessary to take the following thoughts into consideration.

The essential nature of all pre-Christian mysteries was that people aspired to become united with their higher ego, which when they incarnate on the Earth remains in the spiritual world. However, this union was possible for them only outside the physical body and, hence, beyond the confines of their earthly ego-consciousness, which was therefore wholly extinguished for the period of their initiation (a death-like sleep of three days). On returning to the physical body the person undergoing initiation was then able to recall the experiences within the higher ego with the help of his initiators. It was completely impossible for him to take his earthly ego with him into the spiritual world. In the course of the old initiation this was even consistently resisted, because it was considered to be a major impediment to a union with the spiritual world. (This attitude towards the earthly ego continues to be inculcated in certain oriental schools of initiation even today.) Only in this way was it possible for union with the higher ego to take place in the old mysteries.

What took place at the Turning Point of Time was in this respect of an entirely different nature. For the first time there was a situation where man was no longer ascending to his higher ego on the path of initiation but where a divine Being of the highest stature arrived on the Earth who brought with Him the full power of the *true ego*, in order that He might imbue the earthly ego of Jesus of Nazareth with it. This was a process lasting three years, which reached its culmination in the Mystery of Golgotha. Thus a wholly new faculty was implanted into the further course of human evolution. Since then, human beings have, through freely uniting themselves with the Christ impulse, been able to take their earthly ego-consciousness into the spiritual world without in any way impairing it, in order to unite it there with the higher, and subsequently also with the true, ego.

Rudolf Steiner calls this deed of rescue 'the greatest advance that has ever been made, and can ever be made, in the evolution of humanity and of the Earth' (GA 123, 9 September 1910). As a direct consequence of the 'Christ event', that is, of the Mystery of Golgotha, this unique 'advance' now stands at the centre of human evolution and will determine its further progress until the end of the Earth aeon. Rudolf Steiner describes this mighty step, which at the same time signified the transition from the old, pre-Christian to the new Christian mysteries, in which the actual 'development' and 'implementation' of the Christ impulse that has entered earthly evolution will take place, in the following words: 'That aspect of human evolution that we have characterised as the soul's ascent to the realm of spirits, which in pre-Christian times could be attained only within the mysteries and, moreover, only by a certain dulling of the ego in so far as it is developed in ordinary human consciousness, was to receive an impulse whereby this evolutionary stage—which still for the most part belongs to the future of human beings' development—can be attained by man in such a way that as he enters this spiritual world he can fully maintain that ego-consciousness which in our time normally belongs only to the outward plane of the physical world of the senses. This step in human evolution, which was made possible in this way by the Christ event, is the greatest advance that has ever been made, and can ever be made, in the evolution of humanity and of the Earth. That is to say that everything that may still arise in earthly evolution with regard to such a fact is a development, an implementation of the great impulse that has been given through the Christ impulse' (ibid.).

Modern initiation, as we know it today from the legacy of Rudolf Steiner, where man's ego-consciousness remains intact at all stages of his ascent into the spiritual world, could only be established within the new mysteries on the basis of this rescuing of the earthly ego by the Christ impulse. In this way man's earthly ego was for the first time borne in its entirety into the spiritual world and ego-consciousness, the most precious achievement of Earth evolution, could be raised aloft into the sphere of the true ego through its union with Christ.

In his writings on the theory of knowledge, Rudolf Steiner struggled uncompromisingly to point out that since the Mystery of Golgotha man's earthly ego has acquired a position of central significance. Although he does not mention the Mystery of Golgotha in this context, the radical words that he wrote at that time about the significance of the earthly ego only became a possibility because of the consequences of this event for the further destiny of the human ego.

Thus at the end of his essay from 1899 entitled 'Der Individualismus in der Philosophie' (Individualism in Philosophy)—the original title was 'Der Egoismus in der Philosophie' (Egoism in Philosophy)—which appeared in the anthology of articles by various authors on the theme of 'Egoism' with reference to his books *Truth and Knowledge* and *The Philosophy of Freedom*, Rudolf Steiner makes the following observation about the nature of the ego: 'To understand the ego intellectually means to create the foundation for basing everything that derives from the ego also solely upon the ego. The ego that understands itself cannot make itself dependent upon anything other than itself' (GA 30, p. 151). And then he adds these highly significant words: 'After what has been said here it seems almost unnecessary to emphasise that what is meant by the ego can only be the actual, body-bound ego of the individual and not something of a general nature that lies at some distance from him' (ibid.).[44] The immense significance of these words is that one can only speak in such a way about the nature of the earthly ego *since the Mystery of Golgotha*. And anyone wishing to embark on further investigations in the sense of these words as to the source of such an 'actual' and 'body-bound' 'ego of the individual' must sooner or later—if he is to carry out his investigations to the full—arrive at the inner experiencing of the Mystery of Golgotha 'in a most inward, most solemn festival of knowledge' (GA 28, ch. 26), as also occurred in the case of Rudolf Steiner himself at the threshold of the twentieth century.

Hence one can say that it was only because the Mystery of Golgotha had objectively taken place in human history at the Turning Point of Time that Rudolf Steiner was able to speak in the way that he did at that time about the earthly ego and the egotism that has always been associated with it already in his philosophical writings. In his essay 'Der geniale Mensch' (The Person of Genius) (1900) he writes very convincingly in this regard: 'Even if your self widens its horizons to the self of the world, it continues to act in an ego-oriented way' (GA 30, p. 431). The words 'in an ego-oriented way' signify living and working out of one's own ego (the earthly ego).

In other words, since the Mystery of Golgotha it has not been a matter of renouncing the individual ego and, hence, one's own personality but of boundlessly broadening its outlook, so that one assimilates and attends to world-interests as widely and intensively as one otherwise pursues one's own individual passions. Later on in the same essay Rudolf Steiner also calls this the 'ennobling' of one's own self and formulates this aim in a uniquely radical way as follows: 'It is simply not true that a human individual can be selfless. What is, nevertheless, true is that a personal passion can be ennobled in such a way that the person concerned acquires an interest not only in his own situation but in the affairs of all mankind. Do not preach to people that they should be selfless but inculcate in them the highest interests to which this personal passion of theirs, their egotism, can be harnessed'.[45]

For what does it mean if someone renounces his egotism as the necessary foundation of his earthly ego? It means that he will then be renouncing his earthly ego altogether (as is the case with Eastern initiation). If, on the other hand, he broadens his egotism to include the whole of mankind, he is already on the way to uniting his earthly ego with the higher ego, that is, in other words, enabling his ego-consciousness to be received into the sphere of the higher ego in order upon this foundation at some point in the future to become a parti-cipatory element also in the true ego.

Hence in what has been said above there is absolutely no impli-cation of a fundamental renunciation of 'selflessness' but simply that such a quality of selflessness is reached *out of the full power of one's own ego*. For the highest purpose of human evolution on the Earth is served not by cultivating a presumptuous or sentimental attitude at the beginning of the path but by experiencing this purpose to begin with simply as a lofty ideal of the future to which a long, long path will still need to be devoted.

This exalted purpose is, on the modern path of initiation, related to the stage of Intuition, of which a person in ordinary life has knowledge only in the form of the unique instance of the intuition of his ego. Rudolf Steiner writes regarding this in the first section of his book *The Stages of Higher Knowledge*: 'But there is a word that everyone can only address to himself. This is the word "I". No one else can say "I" to me, for every other person I am a "you". Similarly, every other person is for me a "you". Only he himself can refer to himself as "I". The reason for this is that one lives not *outside* but *within* the "ego". Thus through *intuitive* cognition one lives in all things. The perception of one's own "ego" is the model for all intuitive knowledge. In order in this way to form a bond with outer phenomena, one first has to emerge from oneself. One must become "selfless" if one is to be able to merge with the "self", the "ego" of another being' (GA 12, p. 9–10; italics Rudolf Steiner).

These words relate to the fourth stage of modern initiation, where out of the four fundamental elements of knowledge (object, image, concept and 'ego') *the ego* alone remains. (See ibid.) This means that one takes first and foremost one's earthly ego or ego-consciousness, which every human individual possesses on the Earth, with one through all the preceding stages of knowledge into the world of Intuition.

In no sense is there any contradiction between the two questions.

For to the extent that a person is still wholly immersed in himself, that is, lives only in and with his body and is consequently entirely dependent on it, there is no sense in speaking about true selflessness. Such a person simply cannot be selfless. (Were he to endeavour to be so in this state, it would either be an illusion or he would simply lose his ego-consciousness, so that his 'selflessness' would therefore be equivalent to ego-lessness and would accordingly become something behind which no one—as an actual personality—really stands.)

True selflessness, which is born out of the highest development of an ego that has the capacity to merge fully in Intuition with the whole world outside the body, is, in contrast, at the same time the quality for which the only name on the path of initiation is *true* love. Rudolf Steiner says of this: 'Only through the highest development and spiritualisation of the capacity for love can that which manifests itself in Intuition be achieved. It must become possible for man to make the capacity for love into a cognitive power' (GA 227, 20 August 1923).

In the words that have been cited there is already an indication of 'the highest interests' that need to be implanted within human beings in the form of love; for love begins to burgeon forth within the soul with the development of a genuine interest in other beings that ultimately extends to the entire world.

Rudolf Steiner writes of such a love arising from warm interest in all 'objects' of the world in his *Philosophy of Freedom*, where he points out that a free act can only arise from a pure 'love for the object'. (See GA 4, chapter 9.) This follows from what Rudolf Steiner refers to in the same chapter as 'moral intuition' or an 'intuition that is steeped in love'. Only this purely spiritual love ('the power of love in a spiritual form', GA 4, chapter 8), which can be engendered only by the strengthened ego of a human individual, will also as though out of itself bring forth a true selflessness leading not to ego-lessness but having its roots in the ego, which is increasingly able to encompass the whole of the world in love.

★

In order to gain a better understanding of what has actually happened to the earthly ego as a result of the Christ event, one needs to consider certain additional facts arising from spiritual science. In his early discussions of the work of modern philosophers (from Fichte to Bergson) who placed—or attempted to place—the experience of the ego that a person has of it on the Earth at the centre of their philosophy, Rudolf Steiner frequently pointed out that ego-consciousness is interrupted every night. This circumstance specifically demonstrates the inapplicability of Descartes' famous saying, 'I think, therefore I am'; for when one is asleep one is not thinking. One continues, nevertheless, to be an ego-being, otherwise one would not wake up in the morning.

In the following words Rudolf Steiner characterises the problems associated with this together with the ensuing consequences: 'How can it be that we have the phenomenon of that interrupted line of consciousness, whereby our ego-consciousness is being continually broken off [in sleep]? The reason for this is that the notion that we as human beings have of the ego is merely an idea or mental picture of it. And because all mental images sink down as we go to sleep into the darkness of unconsciousness, so also does our idea of the ego. This likewise sinks down into obscurity. The very circumstance that it falls away into oblivion together with the world of mental images shows us that in the ego ... we have a reflection of something that we speak of when we say "I" which does, however, manifest itself to us only in the form of a picture' (GA 137, 7 June 1912).

At the Fourth International Congress on Philosophy in Bologna on 8 April 1911, Rudolf Steiner had also spoken in public about the significance of this quality of the ordinary ego. In the summary that he made of this lecture under the title 'A Statement about Theosophy at the Fourth International Philosophy Congress' he formulated the central thrust of what he had said: 'A future theory of knowledge will recognise that the ego does in truth reside in the outward spiritual world and that the ordinary ego merely serves to reflect its image in the bodily organism' (GA 35).

In his lecturing activity Rudolf Steiner employed many other ways of characterising the earthly ego: the image of the ego, the idea of the ego, the mental picture of the ego, the reflection of the ego; and he frequently equated them with the general activity of earthly ego-consciousness. One can therefore say that the idea of the ego forms the focal point of human ego-consciousness, around which man's conscious life of soul revolves. And when what is perhaps a person's most important idea becomes lost in sleep, his ego-consciousness is likewise immediately extinguished.[46]

As has already been indicated, it follows from Rudolf Steiner's spiritual-scientific lectures that the earthly ego represents a reflection in the body of what he designates as man's higher ego (the gift of the Sun Elohim). The possession of this ego and the ego-consciousness that is engendered by it gives to a human individual on the Earth the only firm point where he is able to distinguish himself as an enclosed, single being from all other kingdoms of nature and feel himself to be elevated above them all. Only through his individual ego-consciousness does a human individual experience himself as such on the Earth; and he is also in need of this same ego-consciousness especially after death, in order fully to remain a human being in the spiritual world. He would otherwise meet with a destiny such as the Greek hero Achilles tells of from the underworld after his death: 'Better to be a beggar in the upper world than a king in the realm of the shades' (Homer, *Odyssey*, 11th Song); for it is the clear ego-consciousness which alone gives a human being on the Earth his human status. In pre-Christian times, on the other hand, even the most significant individuals were threatened with the complete loss of this precious gift of Earth evolution after their death.

Rudolf Steiner then describes in the following words why it was, is and will continue to be so infinitely important for every human individual to take this ego-consciousness with its central focus, the idea of the ego, into the spiritual world: 'The only firm supportive element that a person can bring with him from the Earth into the spiritual world' is his 'idea of the ego' (GA 137, 10 June 1912).

In the old mysteries, however, this was still not possible. The pre-Christian initiate therefore experienced his higher ego as being at the same time in the care of the various hierarchic beings who determine a person's whole path after his death. This was mainly the consequence of the fact that the right of this higher ego to abide with him in the spiritual world could be attained by those seeking initiation only at the cost of the earthly ego (that is, as the result of its obliteration). No human being in pre-Christian times could out of his own resources unite earthly ego-consciousness with his higher ego, which abides in the spiritual world. For this was and is possible for human beings only with help from a particular quarter: 'It is immensely difficult to transfer the idea of the ego from the earthly world to the consciousness into which one enters [in the spiritual world] . . . Help is necessary for this. Without help it cannot be done' (ibid.).

Such help became possible only through Christ since the Mystery of Golgotha. This is the secret that every true Christian initiate knows: 'He knows that this Christ impulse is in our time indeed *the only help* which will not allow us [in the spiritual world] to forget the ego-idea of Earth evolution' (ibid.). Thus through the inclusion of the Christ impulse in modern initiation, the full power of the earthly ego and the individual ego-consciousness that is associated with it is taken with one into the spiritual world, even to its highest levels.

This truth has also found its way into general Christian tradition. Again and again there have been Western thinkers who have drawn attention to the fact that the question of the immortality of the earthly *personality* was raised for the first time in Christian circles. In pre-Christian religions, people spoke only of the immortality of the eternal individuality, namely the higher ego, which goes from one incarnation to another. No particular value was ascribed to ego-consciousness on the Earth as the focal point of the earthly personality, which with every incarnation of a human individual is newly formed from the connection of the higher ego with the physical body. Moreover, it was, as we have already seen, regarded (especially in the Orient) as the main obstacle on the path to higher knowledge.

In contrast, in the occult schools of the Rosicrucians (from the time of their founding in the middle of the thirteenth century) the immortal status of the human personality—which in their writings was referred to as a 'person'—acquired through the Christ event played a central role.[47]

How did this eternal personality come into being? It is possible to form an idea of this through the comparison that Rudolf Steiner draws in his Bologna lecture. According to this man's ego-consciousness is like a reflection of his higher ego, which is thrown back by the physical organism of the body. In ordinary life a person is very clearly distinguished from the appearance of his image in a mirror.[48] For the former belongs to the realm of being, whereas the latter is a mere appearance. A similar relationship also applies to the human ego. The higher ego belongs to the realm of being and ego-consciousness is initially only pure semblance. But at the Turning Point of Time Christ united Himself in His essential nature with this very semblance in the human being Jesus of Nazareth and fully imbued him with the substance of the true ego. As a result this semblance acquired the possibility of partaking in being, that is, it became a new being.

Since then this has been the situation of the whole of man's further evolution on the Earth. For through the deed of Christ the earthly ego has made the transition from the state of semblance to full being. As a result of this, every human being can with the help of the Christ impulse now unite his earthly ego-consciousness firstly with the higher ego and then also with the true ego, in order by virtue of this union to become an independent creator of the future cosmos.[49] It is now possible for a person who has in his earthly ego consciously received the Christ impulse and has accordingly embarked upon the modern path of initiation fully to awake initially in his higher and then in his true ego, in order then to be able to live at all levels of the spiritual world while fully maintaining his individual ego-consciousness and without losing himself in the process.

In the lecture of 12 June 1912 Rudolf Steiner describes how the help of Christ necessary for this is actually experienced by the pupil of the spirit. On the path of modern initiation he reaches a stage where a twofold encounter takes place that he cannot avoid: with Lucifer and death. This encounter is facilitated for the person undergoing initiation at the threshold of the spiritual world by its Guardian. Lucifer then appears to him as the cause of the so-called Fall, whose main consequence is that death makes its appearance in the evolution of mankind. (In the image of the disintegrated form of the human body, death is now made manifest to him.) If, however, the spirit-pupil has already on the Earth attained a deep inner relationship to the Christ impulse, instead of death he sees the Christ, who overcame death in the body of Jesus of Nazareth. And now Christ who appears instead of death shows in what way a human individual can also with the help of Christ maintain his ego in the spiritual world. 'For in the place of death itself, something else appears instead of the disintegrated human body ... In the place of death Christ Himself appears, thus enabling us to understand that this [earthly] ego can after all be preserved' (GA 137). For in the moment when Christ takes the place of death, the earthly ego will no longer die with the body or succumb to unconsciousness (obliteration).[50]

The preservation of the earthly ego therefore becomes the unshakable foundation of the anthroposophical path of initiation and is, as we have already seen, already firmly rooted in Rudolf Steiner's early philosophical writings. In the chapter about initiation in the book *Occult Science*, the first stage of initiation is described as follows: 'The study of spiritual science, whereby one avails oneself initially of the power of judgement that one has acquired in the physical world of the senses' (GA 13, 'Knowledge of Higher Worlds. Concerning Initiation'). This first stage, which gives support and assurance for the entire further path into the spiritual world, would be utterly meaningless if a healthy 'power of judgement', as a significant element and the most important quality of the earthly ego, were to be abandoned or lost at the higher stages of initiation.

Rudolf Steiner goes on to say the following in the same book about the penultimate, sixth stage of initiation, which consists in the spirit-pupil's merging with the entire macrocosm, though without any loss of individual consciousness, that is, without even the slightest loss of his earthly ego: 'He [the spirit-pupil] begins to feel himself in his full independence. This experience is one of reaching out into the whole world and becoming one with it, though *without* losing one's own essential being' (italics Rudolf Steiner).[51]

And then he also adds, while particularly emphasising the importance of fully preserving the human personality (individual consciousness) also for the higher stage of initiation: 'It is significant that this becoming one [with the macrocosm] should not be thought of as if individual consciousness would thereby cease and man's essential nature would flow into the cosmic all' (ibid.).[52]

The highest and—for the present—concluding stage of modern initiation, which in early editions of the book was called 'blessedness in God', appears in later editions in the form of a summary that elevates *all* the previous stages. It is described as 'the combined experience of the previous stages, as a basic soul-mood' (ibid.). Among those 'previous stages' is also the first stage, namely the power of judgement of the earthly ego itself. Thus through his description of modern Christian initiation in this book, Rudolf Steiner creates a mighty bridge between Earth and heaven as a new Jacob's ladder on which man's earthly ego-consciousness unites Earth and heaven in a new way.

In conclusion it should also be mentioned that Rudolf Steiner was a prime example of someone who himself followed the spiritual path described here from the first until the last stage and was through his conscious relationship to Christ able fully to preserve his earthly ego at all levels of the spiritual world, even at the very highest levels. Because of this he had a capacity which no previous initiate has had, namely to present everything that he researched in universally intelligible thought-forms, which through their strict and clear scientific nature are indicative of the distinctive quality of ego-consciousness in the age of the consciousness soul.

We can now also understand the full gravity of the following words which, as Ernst Lehrs reports, Rudolf Steiner spoke in a conversation: 'Marie Röschl once asked Rudolf Steiner whether there was an initiate in his time whose perception extended as high and as far as his own. As she told me later, he answered that there was, but that there was no one with the capacity to clothe what he beheld in the form of thoughts that enable others to comprehend it with their own powers of thinking; for this required bringing what had been spiritually perceived into the brain, and this was a sacrifice that no one else has been able to make.'[53]

Conveying what has been perceived spiritually to the brain is something that only a person's earthly ego is able to do, and, moreover, only if the initiate has previously been able fully to take his ego-consciousness into the spiritual world. Rudolf Steiner's capacity to achieve this to an unprecedented degree is attested by the whole of his

life's work, which in the light of what has been said here is the consequence and the testimony of the direct presence of the power of
Christ in his ego.

Rudolf Steiner's unique significance for the present and future
evolution of mankind consists in the light of the foregoing in that he
was the first who has out of the purest ego-forces been able to attain
the new Christ consciousness, which simultaneously encompasses the
earthly and the spiritual world. Furthermore, he has laid down the
path for our time on which this Christ consciousness can gradually be
attained by every human being.

Notes

All emphases (words or phrases in italics), also in quotations, derive unless indicated otherwise from the author. This also applies to words or phrases in square brackets. Quotations from the Bible are for the most part from the Revised Standard Version, except where Jon Madsen's translation is used to reflect the author's use in such instances of the Emil Bock version.

1. This is the title given to the appendix or addendum concerned in the English translation by Maria St. Goar (see the following note). The reader of the present translation is entitled to a few words of explanation as to why the formulation 'the "I"' as a translation of the German words 'das Ich'—which has, especially in the United States, recently become standard in translations of Rudolf Steiner's work—is not generally employed in the present translation (other than in poetic contexts). The reason is that my experience of the word 'I' in English is of a word that is unwilling to be objectivised, employed referentially or used in any way other than as an expression of individual selfhood. However, a major problem that arises here is that the word 'ego', which is the most widely used alternative, has—despite its well-founded Greek origins—in the experience of many people today become narrowed in its meaning especially through the way that it is defined in Freudian and Jungian terminology. I nevertheless hold the view that it is a word which can still be used as a vehicle for imparting deeper and wider meanings, and in the context of the author's picture of human individuality it is, moreover, wholly appropriate that the word used for this purpose is the one used to refer to the lower, more earthly aspect of our human nature. (Translator's note)

2. *Anthroposophy and The Philosophy of Freedom. Anthroposophy and its Method of Cognition. The Christological and Cosmic-Human Dimension of The Philosophy of Freedom*, Temple Lodge Publishing, Forest Row 2009.

3. Carl Unger, *Gesammelte Werke* (Collected Works), vol. I, p. 305, Stuttgart 1964.

4. The way that the true ego relates to the other (higher) ego and also to the corresponding regions of the spiritual world poses a particular difficulty.

In the last chapter of the book *The Threshold of the Spiritual World* Rudolf Steiner links the true ego mainly with man's life on Higher Devachan. In this sense the 'spiritual world' corresponds to Lower Devachan and the 'super-spiritual world' to Higher Devachan. (See also GA 100, 20 November 1907.) This latter realm can, however, also be related to the other ego, which in the book mentioned above Rudolf Steiner calls the 'spiritual ego-nature'. This 'lives in the totality of the destiny of a human life' (GA 17, chapter 5) and connects all incarnations of a human being in a common unity. 'The course of a person's life is seen to be inspired by his own permanent entity, which continues from life to life' (ibid.). In this way this ego is also the bearer of the whole of a person's karma (ibid.).

This characterisation of the 'other ego' makes it possible to locate its full development in the life after death on Higher Devachan, where life in the higher ego engenders a human being's capacity to attain a complete overview of his former and subsequent incarnations: 'Something of a memory of his earlier lives and a prophetic preview of his future begin to shine forth' (GA 9, 'The Three Worlds: The Spirit in the Spirit-Land after Death').

According to Rudolf Steiner this experience is associated with the Spirit Self. 'That which in this book [*Theosophy*] has been called the 'Spirit Self' lives in this region [Higher Devachan]—in so far as it is developed—in the reality that is appropriate to it' (ibid.).

In order to distinguish this from what has previously been said about the true ego, one needs to bear the following in mind. For the higher ego the realm of Higher Devachan is the realm of its highest development. For the true ego, on the other hand, it is only the lowest realm of its existence. Hence both can be described on *this* level by the spirit-researcher with similar words. However, the true ego extends in its essential nature beyond Higher Devachan to those regions of the spiritual world which lie beyond the 'three worlds' described in the book *Theosophy*. These are those regions which can also be referred to as 'super-spiritual worlds'. (In this sense one can refer to the whole realm of Devachan as the 'spiritual world'.) Here the true ego is connected with the Life Spirit and the Spirit Man, just as the 'other ego' is connected on Higher Devachan with the Spirit Self.

In *Theosophy* the foundation within man for the Life Spirit and Spirit Man is referred to as 'the life-kernel' of his being, which derives 'from still higher worlds' than the three worlds mentioned above (GA 9, 'The Spirit-Land'). The true ego, whose lowest sphere of activity is Higher Devachan, in its essential nature belongs to these 'still higher worlds'.

Something similar can also be said of the cosmic Word to what can be said of the true ego. Its lowest revelation likewise takes place on Higher Devachan, but its real sphere of activity lies much higher, namely, where the true ego also has its origin.

5. It is of significance that in this context Rudolf Steiner uses the name 'real ego' for the higher ego, for the lecture that has been cited here was given in the same year as the publication of the second, enlarged edition of *The Philosophy of Freedom*, where Rudolf Steiner not only made many additions to the text but also re-wrote the beginning of chapter 9 and introduced into this revised version the words 'real ego'. Rudolf Steiner also spoke in the lectures of 19 December 1915 (GA 165) and 1 March 1917 (GA 66) of how man's higher ego does not descend into incarnation.

6. The initiation of many adepts in pre-Christian times was based upon such a conscious connection with the higher or other ego. Above all the figure of Krishna represents a kind of archetype for an initiation of this nature. (See GA 146 and later on in this book.)

7. The way that Rudolf Steiner structures his book *The Threshold of the Spiritual World* so that the three aspects of ego-activity are emphasised is also of significance. Thus the book consists of twelve chapters, which are grouped in three parts of, respectively, three chapters, two chapters and seven chapters, each of which concludes with a 'summary of the foregoing'. Thus in the first summary there is a reference to the earthly ego, in the second summary the other (higher) ego is introduced and in the third summary, which concludes the main content of the book, also the true ego. Likewise in the book *The Spiritual Guidance of the Individual and Humanity* (GA 15), which was published two years beforehand, Rudolf Steiner refers especially in the first chapter—albeit in somewhat different terminology—to the same reality of the three aspects of the ego. There he speaks of 'ego-consciousness' or man's 'conscious self', which gradually awakes after the third year of life (earthly ego). He goes on to speak of the 'expanded' or 'second self', which 'advances ... from incarnation to incarnation'. And finally there is a description of how such an ego leaves the sheaths of Jesus of Nazareth immediately before the Baptism in the Jordan, in order to make way for the other (third) ego as

the 'higher self of humanity which otherwise, without a person's knowledge, works on a child as a force of cosmic wisdom' and which is continually in direct connection with the spiritual world. For Christ came to the Earth as the archetype of every true human ego.

8. Rudolf Steiner also referred to this third Sun as the 'most spiritual' Sun. It is 'the mediator of the highest spiritual forces, the means of connecting the Sun-forces lying beyond the Sun with the inner-solar forces' (GA 266/3, 18 May 1913).

9. The words are given both here and subsequently in Rudolf Steiner's formulation. This is what Paul actually writes in his Letter to the Galatians: '[Yet] I live; and yet no longer I, but Christ lives in me' (2:20).

10. In the esoteric Lesson which has been quoted, Rudolf Steiner used a somewhat different terminology than in the book *The Threshold of the Spiritual World*, where he first introduced the term 'true ego' and gave it a precise definition.

11. In the same lecture Rudolf Steiner refers in the following words to this additional aim of our earthly existence: 'Through the work of our higher ego we transform the transient bodies given to us by the Gods and fashion for ourselves eternal bodies'.

12. Rudolf Steiner speaks about the fully evolved being of man as the religion of the Gods in the lecture of 10 April 1914 (GA 153).

13. Rudolf Steiner speaks of how a knowledge of this esoteric stream of time is 'the precondition for spiritual perception' (GA 262, 'The Barr Manuscript'), which on the path of modern initiation is only possible through the awakening of the higher ego.

14. In the lecture of 4 June 1924 (GA 236) Rudolf Steiner indicates that the time brought to the Earth by Christ from the Sun is that which a human being otherwise 'receives only when he dies'. What is referred to here is the stream of time which flows in the opposite direction to ordinary earthly time (that is, from the future). All hierarchies live and work in the spiritual world within this stream of time, and a person experiences in it the justified consequences of all his former incarnations, on the basis of which he prepares his future earthly lives. Man's higher ego, which passes through all his incarnations and links them in a karmic unity, also lives in this second stream of time.

In the same lecture Rudolf Steiner mentions a third, much higher stream of time which was likewise brought by Christ to the Earth, namely the stream that flows 'from eternity to eternity'. (See further regarding this in the author's book *The Mystery of the Resurrection in the Light of Anthroposophy*, chapter 2, 'Easter, Ascension and Whitsun in the Light of Anthroposophy', English translation, Temple Lodge 2010.) Man's true ego lives and works within this stream. As both of these spiritual streams of time come from the Sun, they also correspond to its twofold nature, that is, respectively its planetary and starry aspects.

Thus in the second part of the Foundation Stone Meditation the transition from the higher ego to the true ego, which culminates in its third part, is already being prepared.

15. See S.O. Prokofieff, *May Human Beings Hear It! The Mystery of the Christmas Conference*, chapter 4, 'The Foundation Stone Meditation in Eurythmy. An Esoteric Study', English translation, Temple Lodge 2004.
16. See further in the author's book *Anthroposophy and The Philosophy of Freedom. Anthroposophy and its Method of Cognition. The Christological and Cosmic-Human Dimension of The Philosophy of Freedom*, chapter 8, 'The Fifth Gospel and Rudolf Steiner's Path of Initiation'.
17. See note 4.
18. In the lecture of 28 March 1910 (GA 119) Rudolf Steiner also refers to this spiritual domain as 'the world of archetypes'.
19. Thus after the union which he had achieved with his true ego, Rudolf Steiner was also able to raise his consciousness to the Buddhi sphere and thus take on the task of a bodhisattva. See regarding this S.O. Prokofieff, *Rudolf Steiner and the Founding of the New Mysteries*, ch. 3, 'The Path of the Teacher of Humanity', English translation, Temple Lodge 1986/1994.
20. It should be added that, in contrast to the bodhisattvas, who ascend from the Earth into the Buddhi sphere on each occasion between their incarnations, Christ Himself descends from the opposite direction, that is, from still higher spiritual worlds to the Buddhi sphere (see GA 116, 25 October 1909). It follows from this that the actual source of the true ego is to be found not in the Buddhi sphere but in still higher worlds.
21. Rudolf Steiner speaks at some length about the twelve world-conceptions in the cycle *Human and Cosmic Thought* (GA 151).
22. Rudolf Steiner speaks of how the twelve pictures of the ego form a 'complete ego' in the spiritual world in GA 119, 29 March 1910.
23. Rudolf Steiner says in this connection: 'In the language of those regions of Western Asia it would have been said of a being such as a bodhisattva while incarnated on Earth that he was "filled with the Holy Spirit"' (GA 114, 20 September 1909).

24. For a further aspect of these three stages of human development, see the end of this chapter.
25. See GA 317, 26 June 1924.
26. See regarding this in S.O. Prokofieff, *Rudolf Steiner and the Masters of Esoteric Christianity* (a translation of this hitherto unpublished book is in preparation) and also in the same author's books *The Cycle of the Year as a Path of Initiation leading to an Experience of the Christ Being. An Esoteric Study of the Festivals*, ch. IX, 2, 'The Exoteric and Esoteric Working of the Etheric Bodies of the Great Initiates in the Twentieth Century', English translation, Temple Lodge 1991/1995 and also *Die geistigen Aufgaben Mittel- und Osteuropas* (The Spiritual Tasks of Central and Eastern Europe), ch. VII, 'Die Mysterien der sechsten Kulturepoche und die Individualitäten der grossen Meister des Westens' (The Mysteries of the Sixth Cultural Epoch and the Individualities of the Great Masters of the West), Dornach 1993/2014 (not hitherto translated).
27. See the motif of the columns in the side panels of the southern green window of the First Goetheanum.
28. One could say that the first interpretation of Paul's words with respect to the threefold nature of human individuality is associated with the modern path of initiation (see page 8), whereas this second interpretation is related to the unique path of Christ Himself at the Turning Point of Time.
29. Thus instead of 'higher ego' one can also say 'ego' here; for the lighting up of the former in man's consciousness signifies that his ordinary ego is imbued with the spiritual power of the higher ego, thus enabling him to arrive at a conscious experience of the spirit.
30. 'The Molten Sea signifies human nature in its pure, unsullied state' (GA 265, p. 435). However, this must be inwardly attained by a human individual if he is to arrive at an experience of his higher self.
31. See ibid. After Hiram plunged into the Molten Sea and had reached the centre of the Earth, he received the Golden Triangle and the Hammer from Cain himself for the future evolution of mankind. The latter symbolises the creative power of the higher ego. Hence in Teutonic mythology the god of the power of the ego, Thor, has the hammer as his tool and his weapon. (GA 121.)
32. In an esoteric context, Rudolf Steiner also indicated the karmic connection between Hiram, Lazarus-John and Christian Rosenkreutz. (See

Hella Wiesberger, 'Rudolf Steiner's research into the Hiram and John individuality' in GA 265.)

33. See especially the lecture of 9 January 1912 (GA 130) and in S.O. Prokofieff, *Die geistigen Aufgaben Mittel- und Osteuropas*, ch. VII, 'Die Mysterien der sechsten Kulturepoche und die Individualitöten der grossen Meister des Westens', Dornach 1993/2014.

34. Compare with what is said on page 52 (note 4).

35. The round brackets are in the original record of the lecture.

36. Because Rudolf Steiner repeats the same thought here, the possibility that the note-taker misheard what he said is very slight, even if one takes the brevity of the notes into account.

37. Hence Rudolf Steiner frequently indicated that it is an important task of anthroposophy to prepare for the sixth post-Atlantean epoch. See, for example, GA 93, 4 November 1904; GA 93a, 5 November 1905; GA 94, 8 July 1906; GA 130, 3 December 1911; GA 159/160, 15 June 1915.

38. See S.O. Prokofieff, *Eternal Individuality. A Karmic Biography of Novalis*, ch. 12, ' "Christ and Sophia". Mysteries of the Sixth Epoch', English translation, Temple Lodge 1992.

39. In several instances Rudolf Steiner uses virtually the same words to describe the birth of the higher ego within man.

40. See regarding this the author's books *May Human Beings Hear It! The Mystery of the Christmas Conference*, the chapter entitled 'Rudolf Steiner and the Karma of the Anthroposophical Society', English translation, Temple Lodge 2004 and *The Occult Significance of Forgiveness*, ch. VIII, 'The Manichaean Impulse in the Life of Rudolf Steiner', English translation, Temple Lodge 1991/2004.

41. The 'Daemon' who inspires him, of whom Socrates had spoken three centuries beforehand, must be understood in the same sense. (See GA 15, chapter 1.) By this means a particular foundation was prepared in Greece for the receiving of Christianity. 'Why did Paul find his best disciples in Greece? Because the ground was prepared there through the influence of Socrates' (ibid.).

42. These words from this lecture given in 1911 undoubtedly have a connection with the following passage in *Occult Science* (GA 13), a book that had appeared the previous year: 'Through this experience the spirit-pupil is initiated into the sublime mystery that is associated with the name of Christ. Christ manifests Himself to him as the exalted *earthly ideal* of man' ('Knowledge of Higher Worlds. Concerning Initiation'). This has to do

with the stage of Intuition in modern initiation, when the first amal-
gamation of the earthly ego (ego-consciousness) with the true ego is
attained. Only when this stage has been completed does the pupil
become aware out of his own experience of the full meaning and higher
significance of the Mystery of Golgotha for the evolution of humanity
and the Earth. 'Once the pupil has in this way arrived through Intuition
at knowledge of Christ in the spiritual world, he will also be able to
understand what took place historically on Earth in the fourth post-
Atlantean evolutionary epoch . . . This is something that the pupil of the
spirit will know from his own experience' (ibid.).

43. 20 May 1908 (GA 103) and 9 October 1905 (GA 93a).

44. It is to Karen Swassjan's credit that he was the first to draw attention to
the particular significance of these words of Rudolf Steiner's. See his
epilogue to the Russian translation of Rudolf Steiner 's essay 'Egoism in
Philosophy', Moscow 2003.

45. It is precisely this primal quality of the earthly ego that the entire Eastern
spiritual tradition (and not only it) has hitherto been unable to understand. In the earthly ego (or the human personality) it sees only the
principal source of egotism. Hence in order to overcome this latter
quality, it seeks to eradicate the earthly ego by all the means available to
it. For the reasons that have already been mentioned, it knows nothing of
the possibility of ennobling the earthly ego and of making it into
something entirely different.

46. That Rudolf Steiner very closely merges the concepts of the idea of the
ego and ego-consciousness becomes apparent from the fact that in his
descriptions of life after death he speaks in the same context of, on the
one hand, the 'idea of the ego' and, on the other, of 'ego-consciousness'.
(See GA 157a, 16 November 1915.)

47. An indication along these lines can be found in the book *Die geheimen
Figuren der Rosenkreuzer aus dem 16ten und 17ten Jahrhundert* (The Secret
Figures of the Rosicrucians from the 16th and 17th Centuries). See Book
1, plates 12, 13, 18 and 19, Altona 1785. Reprinted in Stuttgart, 2006.

48. Only a materialist would make the serious mistake of regarding the
mirror—that is, his physical body—in which merely the reflection of his
being is made manifest as the being itself.

49. Regarding this, see the last chapter of Rudolf Steiner's book *An Outline
of Occult Science* (GA 13).

50. The whole process of the preservation of ego-consciousness by Christ

beyond the threshold of the spiritual world is also associated with the restoring of the phantom of the physical body. However, this aspect of the Christ event cannot be considered here, on the grounds that the present study has to do with the nature of the ego rather than of the body (although they are both inseparably connected with one another in the reality of the Resurrection). The reader can find a full treatment of this second theme in the present author's books *The Mystery of the Resurrection in the Light of Anthroposophy*, English translation, Temple Lodge 2010 and *What is Anthroposophy?*, English translation, Temple Lodge 2006.

51. Since Oriental initiation has no knowledge of any relationship to the Christ impulse, it holds that man's ego-consciousness dissolves at this stage (and actually already much earlier) like a little drop of water in the ocean of the universal spirituality of the world.

52. And then Rudolf Steiner also remarks that if someone were to understand this condition as the loss of his essential nature, this would merely be 'the expression of an opinion emanating from an *unschooled power of judgement*'. From this it follows that a properly developed power of judgement needs to pervade all stages of modern initiation as the most important quality of the earthly ego.

53. Ernst Lehrs, *Gelebte Erwartung*, the chapter entitled 'Hellsehen und Einweihung', Stuttgart 1979.

Bibliography

The following list of Rudolf Steiner's works includes the writings and lectures quoted or referred to in the present book and is arranged in accordance with the numbers of the volumes of the Complete Works (Gesamtausgabe). Especially in the case of lectures, the main intention in compiling this Bibliography has been to indicate where the lectures referred to by the author can be found in English translation.

4   *The Philosophy of Freedom*

9   *Theosophy. An Introduction to the Supersensible Knowledge of the World and the Destination of Man*

10   *Knowledge of the Higher Worlds: How is it Achieved?*

12   *The Stages of Higher Knowledge*

13   *An Outline of Occult Science*

15   *The Spiritual Guidance of the Individual and of Humanity*

16   *A Road to Self-Knowledge. In Eight Meditations*

17   *The Threshold of the Spiritual World*

28   *The Course of My Life/Autobiography*

30   'Methodical Foundations of Anthroposophy: Collected Essays on Philosophy, Natural Science, Aesthetics and Psychology, 1884–1901'. (Not translated as a complete volume.) The essay entitled 'Individualism in Philosophy' has been translated.

35   'Philosophy and Anthroposophy: Collected Essays, 1904–1923'. The Bologna lecture of 8 April 1911 is included in, for example, *Seeing with the Soul*. It can also be found in *Rudolf Steiner's Path of Initiation and the Mystery of the Ego/The Foundations of Anthroposophical Methodology*, Temple Lodge 2013, which includes 'A Statement about Theosophy at the Fourth International Philosophy Conference'.

66   'Spirit and Matter. Life and Death.' (Not translated as a complete volume.)

93   *The Temple Legend*

93a   *Foundations of Esotericism*

94   'Cosmogony. Popular Occultism. The Gospel of St. John (two

courses)'. The lecture of 9 June 1906 is included in *An Esoteric Cosmology*; that of 5 March 1906 can be found in *The Gospel of St John*, Anthroposophical Publications, London 1980. The lecture of 28 October 1906 has not been translated.

99   *The Theosophy of the Rosicrucian / Rosicrucian Wisdom*

100   *True Knowledge of the Christ*

103   *The Gospel of St. John*

105   *Universe, Earth and Man*

112   *The Gospel of St. John and Its Relation to the Other Gospels*

113   *The East in the Light of the West*

114   *The Gospel of St. Luke*

116   *The Christ Impulse*

119   *Macrocosm and Microcosm*

121   *The Mission of the Individual Folk Souls*

122   *Biblical Secrets of Creation / Genesis*

123   *The Gospel of St Matthew*

125   *Paths and Goals of the Spiritual Human Being*

127   'The Mission of the New Spiritual Revelation'. (Not translated as a complete volume.) The lecture of 25 February 1911 is translated under the title 'The Work of the Ego in Childhood' *(Anthroposophical Quarterly 21:4)*.

130   *Esoteric Christianity*

131   *From Jesus to Christ*

137   *Man in the Light of Occultism, Theosophy and Philosophy*

142   *The Bhagavad Gita and the Epistles of St. Paul*

143   'Experiences of the Supersensible'. (Not translated as a complete volume.) The lecture of 17 December 1912 is available under the title *Love and its Meaning in the World*.

146   *The Occult Significance of the Bhagavad Gita*

147   *Secrets of the Threshold*

151   *Human and Cosmic Thought*

153   *The Inner Nature of Man and Our Life between Death and a New Birth*

157a   *The Forming of Destiny and the Life after Death*

159/160 'The Mystery of Death'. (Not translated as a complete volume.) The lecture of 15 June 1915 is available separately under the title *Preparing for the Sixth Epoch*.

165   *Unifying Humanity Spiritually*

187   *How Can Mankind Find the Christ Again?*